Praise for Servet Hasan's

Tune Him In, Turn Him On

"A powerful aid to a woman's sense of herself in relationship to men."

—Marianne Williamson, *New York Times* bestselling author of *The Age of Miracles*

"I love this book! Every woman should read it, young or senior. Reading this book years ago would have made relationships a lot easier."

—Terry Cole-Whittaker, author of *What You Think of Me Is None of My Business*

"Lively and funny, and based on the premise that women need to take control of their relationships, this is a terrific book."

—*New Age Retailer*

the
INTUITIVE HEART
OF
ROMANCE

Paul Gregory

About the Author

Servet Hasan's varied career began in fashion, writing, and event planning, but her thirst for spiritual knowledge grew, eventually transporting her to Tibet, and later India, where she met the Sai Baba. Encouraged to seek the path of enlightenment, she spent years studying with the mystic masters of the Far East. She has made it her life's work to share these powerful messages with millions through television and radio appearances, live seminars, workshops, and books.

Servet is also a clairvoyant and medium, a gift passed down to her through many generations. She is the author of *Exercises for the Mind* and *Tune Him In, Turn Him On*, as well as a monthly column, "Inside His Head," that runs locally in Orange County, California.

Born in Pakistan, Servet is also a citizen of Great Britain, Canada, and the United States. She considers herself a citizen of the world. For more information, please visit www.servethasan.org.

the

INTUITIVE HEART

OF

ROMANCE

FINDING YOUR OWN PATH
TO LASTING LOVE

SERVET HASAN

Llewellyn Publications
Woodbury, Minnesota

First Edition
First Printing, 2011

Cover design by Ellen Lawson
Cover image © iStockphoto.com/yewkeo
Editing by Nicole Edman

Llewellyn Publications is a registered trademark of Llewellyn Worldwide
Ltd.

Library of Congress Cataloging-in-Publication Data
Hasan, Servet.
  The intuitive heart of romance: finding your own path to lasting love /
Servet Hasan.—1st ed.
     p. cm.
  ISBN 978-0-7387-2584-0
  1. Man-woman relationships. 2. Mate selection. 3. Love.
4. Intuition. I. Title.
  HQ801.H35267 2011
  646.7'7—dc22
                                         2010026990

Llewellyn Worldwide Ltd. does not participate in, endorse, or have any authority
or responsibility concerning private business transactions between our authors and
the public.
  All mail addressed to the author is forwarded but the publisher cannot, unless
specifically instructed by the author, give out an address or phone number.
  Any Internet references contained in this work are current at publication time,
but the publisher cannot guarantee that a specific location will continue to be
maintained. Please refer to the publisher's website for links to authors' websites
and other sources.

Llewellyn Publications
A Division of Llewellyn Worldwide Ltd.
2143 Wooddale Drive
Woodbury, MN 55125-2989
www.llewellyn.com

Printed in the United States of America

The power of intuitive understanding will protect you
from harm until the end of your days.

—LAO-TZU

CONTENTS

List of Exercises   *xiii*
With Deepest Gratitude   *xv*
Preface   *xvii*

Introduction:
Redefining Relationships 1

PART I

Sacred Self:
Staying in the Center of Your Own Life

1: Getting Out of Your Own Way. 15

  Staying Centered   20
  Opening Your Heart   26
  Tune In to Yourself First   34
  Effort versus Struggle   41
  You Are Not Here to Fix or Change Anyone   45

Guaranteeing You Will Have a Committed
    Relationship   48

2: Shining the Light on Your Darkness. 51

The Masks We Wear   60
Tell Me Your Story, and I'll Tell You Mine   66
Hidden Fears Over Commitment   69
Ms. Overly Independent   73
Patterns That Plague Us   79
Releasing Repression   87
Shining Your Light   91

3: Relinquishing Fears 97

Fear versus Intuition   102
Hidden Holes   104
The True Meaning of Forgiveness   106
Call In the Troops   108
Turn Your Back on Other People's Fear   113

PART II

Sacred Joining:
The Divine Dance of You, Me, We

4: Seven Steps to Karmic Communication 119

Step 1: The First Chakra (Root)—Red   125
Step 2: The Second Chakra (Spleen)—Orange   126
Step 3: The Third Chakra (Solar Plexus)—Yellow   128

Step 4: The Fourth Chakra (Heart)—Green   130

Step 5: The Fifth Chakra (Throat)—Blue   132

Step 6: The Sixth Chakra (Forehead)—Indigo   134

Step 7: The Seventh Chakra (Crown)—Violet   136

5: Spiritual Conflict Solving 143

Fighting Fair   155

The Blame Game   161

Love *Does* Mean Having to Say You're Sorry   162

Don't Ask, Don't Tell   164

What's Not Working and Why   165

The Cost of Compromising   168

Cosmic Communication   170

What Do Men Really Want?   173

When Do You Know You Should Leave?   175

Axe the Ultimatum   178

6: Learning to Trust Your Intuition 183

Some Basic Truths   189

Developing Your Senses   194

Yes, But . . .   194

The Answer Is in the Aura   200

Color My Aura   203

PART III

Sacred Union:
The Spiritual Path to True Love

7: Sacred Sex 209

    What's Love Got to Do with It?   217
    Set the Stage   220
    Let Loose   220
    How to Have a Better Orgasm   223

8: The New "I Do" 227

    The Myth of Marriage   233
    Creating Your Relationship Affirmation   236
    Real Love Stories   238

9: How to Kill a Commitment, or the Number One
Mistake Women Make 241

    You Are Power-Ful!   251

Conclusion:
Bless Each Other and Bless the World 255

EXERCISES

Grounding Meditation 25
Hand On Your Heart Meditation 33
Creating a Sacred Space 37
Staying Solid as a Rock 44
Write from the Heart 78
Clearing Meditation 85
The Three-Dimensional Vision Board 89
Things That Will Help Your Light Shine 93
Making Friends with Your Fear 104
Sweet Surrender 112
Give Your Fear Away 115
Clearing the Chakras Meditation 138
Start a Relationship Journal 151
Intuitive Dating 159
Superstar Impressions 193
Protecting Your Aura 204
Sexercises 225
Have a Counsel Meeting with a Powerful Woman 250

WITH DEEPEST GRATITUDE

To my parents, for not only giving me the gifts they have given me, but for teaching me to use them wisely and trust them. I love and appreciate you both.

To my daughter, Sabrina—may you continue to reinvent romance for the rest of eternity. I am so proud of the strong, independent woman that you have become. I love you more than words.

Most especially, to the love of my life—I thank you for giving me the greatest gift of all ... your heart. I will forever hold you warmly in mine.

To my best friend and soul sister, Sandy Rodrigues, for her wise insights, endless sense of humor, honesty, and her profoundly generous and loving heart. I am honored to have you in my life. To Mark, her husband, who has been hijacked into my family whether he likes it or not. Thank you, Mark, for being there.

To Paul Hooks, just for being Paul Hooks. You will forever keep me grounded and humbled. I bow to you, my friend.

A special heartfelt thanks to Carrie Obry at Llewellyn Publishing for her invaluable detailed suggestions when helping to shape the manuscript and for allowing me to blossom as a writer. Carrie, your enthusiasm was, and is, positively contagious.

And, a humongous bouquet of sunflowers to my teacher and dear friend, Terry Cole-Whittaker, for being the guiding light and road map on my spiritual journey. Your vision brought me to where I am. I hope that I will forever make your heart smile, as you do mine.

Last, but not least, to anyone seeking love on a spiritual path: may you love and be loved.

SERVET

PREFACE

When I began writing my first relationship book, *Tune Him In, Turn Him On*, something amazing happened to me. I met someone new. Yes, the book really does work! In case you need further proof, this was after some statistics stated that at my age I had a better chance of being struck by lightning or killed by a terrorist than finding true love. Lovely. But not only did I meet a man, I met *the* man. The man of my dreams.

I saw him coming, but I didn't trust my intuition and doubted if he would make it to my side. But somehow he did, and he quickly set about awakening me from a deep, dark sleep. With every embrace my nightmares disappeared and with every kiss my soul smiled. I found true love.

Did it scare me? Yes! So much so that I was paralyzed with fear. I said I wanted true love, but at the same time, I had done everything in my past to avoid it. Lurking somewhere in the dark corners of my subconscious mind, I held the insidious belief that if I allowed someone in, I might lose everything—I might lose myself. I had made my own life, you know, and I hesitated on the edge of this precipitous cliff, wondering if I could go to the moon and keep the stars. I used to think I didn't have enough time to do everything I wanted to do and still love a man. To me, surrendering to love meant that I would have to give up myself so he could shine.

However, the landscape of relationships has changed drastically over the past few decades. More and more women are choosing not to marry, and many opt to remain childless. A woman's role in this world has far surpassed the dynamics of predefined societal parameters to include much more than was previously acceptable. As a result, women have had to renegotiate their terms of partnership, especially after centuries of suppression. But men have to figure out the new setup as well. We are *both* learning our new roles, in marriage and in society. This being the case, we have to show up enough to give the guy, and ourselves, a chance. There's a whole new world out there now, with new possibilities for union and equality. The emergence of true feminine power and glory—while not easy and very much a work in progress—has made it less complicated to love a man. Yes, to some degree, a relationship does force us to surrender our sense of separateness, but not in a bad way—in a more enlightened way that actually makes us stronger and more powerful.

When it comes to union and equality, limitless possibilities exist, each as unique as the people involved. A kind of renegotiation for partnership has come into play where we can rethink, redesign, and recast our romantic ideals from a spiritual perspective rather than a worldly one imposed on us by society. And from this new paradigm emerges a whole new definition of commitment.

My mother and father had an arranged marriage in India. She was twelve and he was fifteen. Neither laid eyes on each other until after the ceremony. Growing up I watched my mother take on a subservient role in life. My father had been taught to treat a woman as property and my mother had been taught to accept that. They have been married for over sixty years and I now know they are happy, but watching my mother be submissive didn't exactly leave me anxious to go for a walk down an aisle. I was about as commitment phobic as you could get.

Despite it all, I still longed to break down the walls around my heart and find a lasting, loving relationship. And I did, but only after I understood that the only person I had to be true to was myself.

A stereotypical relationship would not work for me. This much I knew. I longed for something pulsing with life, something alive, vital, and dynamic. I wanted to move from separateness to oneness without losing myself or my freedom. Only in this context could I create a partnership that remained free from expectations and illusions, which I convinced myself created nothing but dullness and boredom. So I listened to my intuition and I took a chance...a chance on love. I cast my fate in the direction of my heart

If I join with you, will I survive?
Take the journey, he said.
From whence you came was not real.
It is the land of death, of dying.
Take the journey, he said.
Come with me, and let me love you.
And you will live forever.

and reached for what was truly mine. I decided that although the ride may not be smooth, I would get on that roller coaster. I breathed in love and exhaled heaven—and I shall never regret it as long as I live.

It began with two people who had the conscious understanding that the purpose of our union was to surpass the material earthly plain and delve head-on into the realm of the spiritual. We could remain independent, dependent, and interdependent, but only if we made that commitment to ourselves first. It came down to finding the center of who I am, and the center of who he is, so that we could discover who we would become together.

The enlightened journey I set out on taught me to forget the lies I had been told, forget what I had been taught to believe, forget the ideas that had been outgrown by society, much less by me. I banished the mind and the brain. Instead, I opened my heart and, by using my own intuitive and psychic abilities as guidance, moved directly into the flow. I found that this was the only way to reach beyond the realm of this world and enter the land of infinite possibility. And when I did, I climbed higher and faster to a place filled with peace, happiness, and bliss.

This book is not about rules for creating intimacy, or even a "marriage made in heaven" (whatever that is). What this book will do is take you beyond the how-to's and manipulations of a so-called formula filled with rules and regulations, and show you how to create real spiritual bonds that last a lifetime.

Because I took the journey into this magical and mystical world I now know, with all of my heart, that you can too. You own the power. By fully expressing yourself in all of your many dimensions, you can stand firm and whole as an individual and have exactly what your heart desires by following the spiritual path to love. Allow me to show you the way into the intuitive heart of romance.

introduction

REDEFINING RELATIONSHIPS

Everything contains everything else.

—THICH NHAT HANH

As an intuitive spiritual counselor and reverend, one of the most common questions I hear from women (after, "When will I meet the man of my dreams?") is "Will this relationship go anywhere?"

I have counseled thousands of women through my workshops, seminars, radio, television, and private intuitive readings for over two decades, and no matter how deep into the trenches I go, I continually draw on the fact that we are all spiritual beings who possess six, not five, senses.

Unfortunately, it's in our relationships—most especially attracting love and sustaining it—that most women struggle the most. *I must have been completely blind to not see this person as he really was. I felt so sure that this time, I would work it out with this man. We loved each other like crazy, but after awhile all we did was argue. He seemed so perfect, and I thought we'd be happy, but it faded so quickly.*

I hear these statements, or some version of them, over and over again. I'm no longer surprised that the women asking are usually bright, attractive, intelligent, and ready to love. Often, they've been in relationships where they thought the man was "the one," only to discover that he wasn't taking the initiative and moving the relationship to the next level. Shaken, they step back, which often leads to anger, not only at themselves, but at their potential partner. One party or the other might end the relationship without really knowing why. Either way, it's over, and once again, she's coming back with the same two questions above.

Helping my clients and witnessing their ability to move beyond this emotional roller coaster has been the greatest experience of all. My job is to help women realize just how patient the Universe can be. If we don't "get" a lesson, you can bet your next paycheck that it will repeat itself. Only when we dig deeper into the core of our being can we realign ourselves by using our intuition to enrich our existing relationships and stop the situation from happening again. Then you not only attract what you want, you discover exactly what that is in the first place.

The approach I use combines Eastern philosophy with spirituality. Born in Pakistan, my ancestors passed down a natural gift to divine the future. It started at a young age at the kitchen table when my mother taught me to read palms and decipher the messages revealed to us by the leaves in a tea cup. Although my gift evolved naturally and through self-teaching, I still struggled to find the true meaning of life and the soul's evolution. For the next thirty years, I devoted myself to studying religion and mysticism.

In India, I had the privilege of working hands-on with several masters, where I harvested a bountiful supply of rich spiritual truths. They taught me the profound significance of every thought we think, of every word we utter, and every mood we indulge in. Through them, basic universal laws became my guide to the intrinsic nature of our souls.

But my real education began when I started doing the intuitive readings themselves. This made me realize that our psychic sense *is* a spiritual sense. By marrying the two within our heart and soul, we can fulfill any desire we have. Understanding spiritual concepts is one thing, but it was through demonstrating how to gain psychic confidence that I could finally help people bridge the gap from their confusion and insecurities to the soul-centered self that brings meaning and balance back into their lives. Through their intuition, they learned the same step-by-step program I share with you here, and they transformed love into a natural state of being.

As humans we are constantly changing, shifting, and growing; consequently, so are our relationships. When we enter a new stage of love, our psychic gifts become vital tools for gaining more clarity about our self and our partner, giving us insight into what should be a grand and passionate romantic adventure. The perspectives gained by opening your intuitive channels will gently move you through the three phases that any lasting relationship entails—Sacred Self, Sacred Joining, and Sacred Union.

When we begin with our Sacred Self, we look within to find what we want without. You will acquire the intuitive tools necessary to move into the center of your being by clearing away past and present obstacles, for we cannot really love another until we love ourselves. With practices such as meditation, grounding, and clearing, we become aware of our behavior, of the choices we make, and of the attitudes we own. When we learn to make space for love inside our own heart, that space will be filled.

In Sacred Joining we take on a deeper level of understanding and compassion that allows us to see our partner more clearly, free of illusions. We wake up, remain present, and can adjust our intense emotional reactions and fears. Conflicts are handled naturally by delving beyond the physical into our deeper karmic connections. Through our chakras, auras, and our ability to communicate on a spiritual, telepathic level, we come together equally and freely to dance the dance that makes us a couple. When we nest within our own mind, we will build a home for two.

Only then can we move into Sacred Union, a state in which we create a loving, trusting bond with our beloved. With spiritual tools such as crystals, auras, and even feng shui for better sex, we follow the current of the river flowing through our romantic lives easily and effortlessly to create intimate unions that lift us up and propel us forward into heightened perceptions and pleasures beyond anything we imagined existed—a love that is so magical and mystical, you are quite literally drunk with an elixir that permeates every cell in your body. When we make a home within our own soul, it will be settled.

By accessing our intuitive tools, we no longer live in fear, feeling powerless and inadequate. We heal our emotional wounds and mend our uncertain heart. It's a navigational system that cannot and will not fail you. My goal has never been to write a book that claimed it had the answer, but to guide you to find the answer within yourself. Your destiny is written on your soul; by using your intuition, you can claim it any time you want. Throughout the book, I'll give you real-life examples of how my clients learned to use their sixth sense to change and improve their lives.

These are not quick fixes, but, quite frankly, they are miraculous. As you move through each phase you will find that you are no longer concerned about the form of the relationship, but the context. Form is wanting to make a relationship fit your picture of what you *think* it should be, whether it's good for you or not, rather than allowing it to evolve organically into its own design, without our interference.

You see, it's when we refuse to give up one way of getting what we want that we push intimacy further away. It's a no-win situation, because all we are trying to do is reconcile the irreconcilable. Instead of allowing our ego, judgment, and fear to come into play in order to satisfy our programmed and conditioned needs (which usually involves a hidden agenda with ulterior motives), we honor our intuitive self and reinvent relationships that work for everyone's higher good. It's not the love you get that counts so much as the love you give. If you want to create a lasting bond, this transformation can only begin within.

When you transform from within, you flow easily from separateness into oneness, because you based your intimacy on understanding and compassion. You stop hiding from yourself and those you love; you create your own path to lasting love. Believe this, and you can change your world.

As we attune to both ourselves and our partner, we naturally begin to ask questions like, "Who is he?" and "Who am I?" If you passionately embrace what he feels, needs, and wants and what you feel, need, and want, you transcend mere togetherness and enter the realm of true union. Self-awareness, commitment, openness, acceptance, shared values, and the ability to handle conflict (all of which we will discuss) are what allow the relationship to transcend earthly predictability into one that works for your higher good, and his. In the intuitive heart of romance we experience loving another person while remaining completely at peace with ourselves.

In this new context, commitment is no longer a material aspect of a relationship, but a spiritual one. One in which two people take a bold and masterful step into the heart of each other, to lift themselves above and beyond any physical or practical or sociological constraints, and find heaven on earth.

That's because intuition strips away the veils of illusion in life, revealing nothing but the truth. It is a faculty of your spirit and, therefore, surpasses an emotional point of view. Relationships are where we resist this the most, because love pushes all of our buttons, on our most vulnerable level. To avoid this, the relationship must begin within our own center. Otherwise fear sets in, fear of being swallowed up by another. Our natural inclination then is to hold back, giving halfway while keeping one foot in the relationship and the other out. People sense that you are not giving fully, and when they do, the relationship often ends before it even begins.

Looking outside ourselves for security, validation, or self-worth puts you in the world of illusion. Metaphysically, this is referred to as the "fall of man." In biblical terms this is where Adam and Eve ate the apple, but that's a whole other story. The fall, however, is still the same. One begins to believe that they aren't "enough" as they are, that unless someone loves them and gives meaning to their life, they are not worthy. No one's worth is based on anything outside of themselves; it all starts and ends with our own soul. Love is an art form, just like writing, music, painting, dancing, acting, and all the rest. You cannot hold back, or you will not thrive. If that's true, then in the end, the only relationship you're really having is with yourself and your source.

Whether we realize it or not, the only door into the intuitive heart of romance is through another person's soul, and the only way to reach their soul is to blend it with your own. It's almost alchemical, in that the conversion of the two creates a substance that is entirely new. An intermingling of two bodies, two minds, two hearts that can resonate simultaneously yet autonomously to create an experience of the vastness of love that surpasses any physical bond. We become one person. This should never be taken lightly. Some people just don't know how deep intimacy can go. It reaches the core, the very being of not only another body, but your own.

When you use your intuition, you will not only attune to yourself, but to your partner. Whether it's through a simple gesture, a smile, a touch, a certain look, or sheer silence, you will automatically know the answer to how the relationship is progressing. Your connection entwines together through moment-to-moment awareness. You not only feed each other's minds and bodies, but each other's spirit. This is how we lift each other up and continually make each other better people, better than we would be alone.

Some people say that falling in love is a delusion. Well, if that's true, I say make me delusional. It's not denial; in fact, it's the exact opposite—an agreement to be ourselves. When we are in love, we become better at romance, at intimacy and can truly have a real commitment, not because we got better at relationships, but because we got better at being human.

What defines a commitment to another person starts and ends with a commitment to yourself. If you are accepting of who you are, then you and your partner create a context of trust and safety. You become a safe harbor, where love can be expressed freely and honestly. This is the only way to find your own path to lasting love.

I cannot offer quick Band-Aid solutions to "catching" a man, getting him to walk you down the aisle, and putting an "I do" into his mouth. But I can offer the spiritual and intuitive tools necessary to make a truly deep connection. If you choose to take this challenge, you automatically change how you think, the choices you make, and the attitudes and perspectives you take on. You change the rules of relationships by moving out of your head and into your heart—the intuitive heart of romance.

SACRED SELF

Staying in the Center of Your Own Life

You yourself, as much as anybody in the universe,
deserve your love and affection.

—THE BUDDHA

1

GETTING OUT OF YOUR OWN WAY

The problem comes when we want to cling to a particular
thought or idea. The mind always wants to cling.

—RAM DASS

When Cupid's arrow first hits, it not only pierces your heart, it pierces your brain. Personally, I went crashing straight into love. Not unlike most people, I was completely overwhelmed by a rush of excitement and euphoria laced with romantic ideology. I felt like a drug addict who simply couldn't get enough of the high. As a result, I walked into a glass wall, missed a ten-car train that came and left right in front of my eyes, stepped into the shower fully clothed ... I could go on and on.

But eventually the biological and chemical reactions that produced the instant gratification, which scientists proved cause the same chemical reaction as taking cocaine, wore off. Left with a bad hangover, I was forced to step back and determine whether the relationship would end or deepen into something that makes even the stars in the sky seem brighter.

But I hesitated. I didn't commit as quickly as he did. Unconsciously, I was waiting to see how he would react before I jumped in with both feet. The truth is that it wasn't fair to me, or to him. Whatever we refuse to acknowledge in ourselves is reflected back to us, and what we condemn in others, we attract to ourselves. I was holding back. In fact, what I was doing was preparing myself for the relationship to end, and by so doing, not allowing it to really begin. What was I so afraid of?

My sixth sense has always been my greatest gift. I believe that intuition is a spontaneous reaction of our soul and, if we allow this substance to bubble up from within our deepest core, we cannot help but find happiness. Of course, I meditated, and tuned into my higher consciousness. By listening to my intuitive self, I realized that I can never feel lost or alone and that I will always be guided and shown the best possible direction for my personal growth and well-being. With a grateful heart, I knew that around every corner an angel awaited, and she carried with her any answer I needed.

Staying true to my beliefs, I discovered that, now that I had found the perfect partner, it was imperative that I maintain my own integrity and self-esteem. On a spiritual level, it became crucial that I rely on my own intuition and allow myself to be guided by spirit, not by the ego. Without discerning this inner life, I was being tossed around on a tidal wave of hysterical emotions. Only by finding my spiritual center and moving within my inner world, rather than the outer world, could I experience lasting love. This is the true meaning of Sacred Oneness. We stay in the center of our own life even while joining hands with another soul. We look at the world through the same set of eyes. If we see demons, we know we can fight them.

If we feel weakness, we know we will find strength. If we see fear, we know we can transform it. Through these psychic eyes, I saw that the stars would guide me, and its gentle breeze would carry me through any challenges I faced.

Once that commitment permeated my being, I felt secure enough to give myself fully to him without fear and to remain whole within the relationship itself. Finally, I chose to accept the possibility of limitless possibilities and moved forward with the relationship, and I am happy to say that he did too. We both committed to making a commitment. In order to grow and thrive, we knew we had to step up to a higher level of participation and assume the responsibility of becoming an intimate partner.

"I can't go on living without you," was no longer a feeling to hide from and not admit, but an understanding that this love would not take us down; it would lift our spirits so we could fly. It is a place where we could say, "Heal me and I'll heal you," and together we can both heal the world.

Most of us try to navigate the path alone, which eventually results in some sort of panic attack. Am I doing it right? Is this fair? Is this meeting my needs? Am I meeting someone else's needs? Can I express myself? Are there appropriate boundaries? Are there too many boundaries?

If we neglect our spiritual center, where our intuition resides, we will naturally get caught up in these material aspects of love. When we find that loving place within us, honesty can prevail. We tell the truth but will also listen to it, without condemnation or judgment. We lose the fear and have more faith in the ability to heal than in the fear that would have us run away or push them away. Love will continually renew us, but fear will only tear a relationship apart. I did the inner work and mended my broken psychic bones. This shifted the energy from a sense of urgency to the compassion, care, and kindness of truly bonding with another soul.

Staying Centered

By definition, intimacy involves more than one person. But to me, the true meaning of the word involves a growth within. Initially, we must move out of separateness into the world of our Sacred Self alone. We must take off the masks we have hidden behind and discover, on a most elemental level, not only who we really are, but who we want to become.

Intimacy is where we are willing to move so deeply into love that we are unafraid of facing the demons that deter us from our conviction to find the light. When the darkness comes, we stand up and face it head on with the steadfast knowledge that if we don't, we will merely repeat the process, with this same person or with someone else. It involves placing romance into the same category as your intuitive practice.

This demands authentic engagement, one where agreements are honored and false moralities denied. We cut through the defenses we've built up over a lifetime so that in the end, we are more fully present. It's an adult ideal, but that's because it's not for amateurs. There is no simple way to pass through the initiation of our hardened hearts and crushed souls to a place where we can say, Yes, I am up for the challenge. When you take that courageous leap, then true love appears to greet you and kicks the devil in the butt. When you don't do it right, it ends in pain.

A relationship then, becomes a fearless exploration of who we are. In order to do this, we must reopen our psychic wounds by confronting all of our fears and anxieties with openness and honesty. Manipulation, deceptiveness, and a willingness to make compromises we know are not in our own better interest take a back seat because we are no longer attached to a specific goal. We no longer run away, tell lies, or become deceptive or manipulative. Instead, we take our fears out, buy them a martini, and become lifelong friends. Knowing our fears makes it much easier for us to accept them, and only by accepting them will we ever transcend them.

I'm not kidding myself, or you, by implying that this is all a piece of cake. It's not. I know it can be hard to take responsibility for your life. But look at it this way: if you aren't responsible, then it means someone else is. And if someone else has control, they may or may not fix your issues. However, if *you* have control of your Sacred Self, you can change anything, anywhere, anytime you like. So fess up. No more whining or complaining. You found a man by doing the work on yourself, and the same work can move you into a relationship that can and will last a lifetime, *if* that's what you truly want.

Whether it is or not is immaterial. I still believe that all women deserve rich, emotional, intimate lives. But in order to do that, we first have to wake up to our own genius, our own power, and then use it wisely. We must learn thoroughly our female self, by allowing our strengths to shine. And the only way to do this is to truly express what's in our heart and on our mind. In my opinion, female power has nothing to do with political issues. Female power comes from taking a stand—emotionally, physically, psychologically, and spiritually—for what you believe in without fear of judgment or punishment. In the end, women's issues are nothing more than human issues.

So, we must treasure who we are and invest in that person. Remember, there's a huge difference between being self-centered, and being self-investing. The first one originates from the ego, the second from the spirit. When we walk with spirit, we have an inner radiance that emanates from our center, affecting everyone we encounter in a positive way.

This inner growth takes a concerted effort, but it's your intuition that opens the space for that magic to occur. Once we master this, we begin to understand ourselves and recognize all the faces and forms that an ecstatic joining involves.

Wherever you are... there you are. We are all here, somehow. Start looking at the conditions and events in your life without emotional judgment. Use your intuition to objectively study how you got where you are. We are responsible only for ourselves. We do not cause, and are not responsible for, anything anyone else does or says.

For so many women, the idea of being true to themselves has been submerged beneath strict indoctrination in a rigid set of beliefs and behaviors we inherited from our parents. Rather than developing our own set of values based on experience and observations, we bought into what we were taught. Under these rules and regulations, we drifted farther and farther away from ourselves. Your karma got run over by your dogma, so to speak.

But to create the perfect partnership, we need enough of a separate self so we are not afraid of being swallowed up or absorbed by the other person. If you want to know what a man's dream is, it's no different than yours: he wants to be himself. And you want to be you. If you do not hold a space for that within each other, you cannot know him and he cannot know you. And to know each other is to know love.

When we feel secure, we give ourselves fully to another without fear of being absorbed, thus remaining whole within the relationship. We become unattached to the scripts and fantasies we contrived in order to find fulfillment, which left us frustrated, disappointed, and ultimately lonely, even if we were with someone at the time. Our demanding ego no longer shouts out orders—You should be doing this! or giving me that! or becoming this person! We feel that if it's not our way, we can't function, alone or together. And does that approach work? Well, no.

The foundation for a healthy, loving relationship is two well-formed people who can be separate, yet able to merge into union with each other. Long-term couples have learned to weave their lives together with the threads of their different temperaments, needs, interests, energies, passions, fears, and desires. They do this by staying centered on who they are in order to meld two separate identities into one.

Too often women are their own worst enemies. They mold themselves to fit the situation or circumstance in order to make things work. The ego mind wants us to believe that we can make such things happen, but spiritually, you can't make anything happen from this level of thinking. Intuitively, immerse yourself in the stream of life. Feel the rhythmic passions dancing through you and you will create new vitality within any relationship.

When you come from the center of your being, you intuitively shift toward oneness. Here, everything becomes a form of energy, moving within us and between us. We are permeated by our partner's being, and he with ours. It is only an illusion that we are separate, one the ego entertains through our insecurities and fear. As we become conscious of this profound level of oneness, we become exquisitely aware of a meaningful connection. We know what to say and what to do. Every action and reaction will be backed by this innate, intuitive energy, leading us exactly where we want to go.

In self-acceptance we feel steady, natural, and unafraid. That's because our ability to love another will always be dependent on our ability to love ourselves.

Kahlil Gibran writes in *The Prophet*, "In our giant self lies our goodness, and that goodness is in all of us. Loving-kindness is like bringing a vast embrace to all we are and feeling the radiance at the center of our being."

EXERCISE

Grounding Meditation

In a relationship it is easy to be excessively influenced by someone else's vibrations. If you are anxious, nervous, short-tempered, volatile, or emotional, you need to stop, balance yourself, and ground.

Stand in a comfortable place, preferably with the earth beneath your feet. Place your arms by your side and turn your palms upward. Exhale and inhale to the count of four. Now imagine all of your energy shifting downward through your body into the ground. Repeat this until you feel calm.

Now place your faith in a higher source. I believe with all my heart that there is a God, and I also believe He's smarter than you or I. I put my faith and trust in this. What this then allows me to do is to step back from a fear or negative belief, which is nothing more than a form or energy, and realize that it is based primarily on memories of the past. Whether you call it God, Spirit, the Universe, or another name doesn't matter. A powerful way to access this is simply to ask abstract questions such as, "What does happiness mean to me?" or "What does love mean to me?"

When we do this, we breathe space between our beliefs, feelings, and wants. Finally, you can smile at the drama of your life and see your own part in creating it. As you ground yourself in experience rather than thought, you can see the forest for the trees, so to speak. It's a simple place, a quiet place, where you can then look into your lover's eyes and ask, "Is this the person I want to have a passionate, romantic, and sacred adventure with?" and know the right answer will come to light, even if it's midnight and dark outside, as well as inside.

If you are spiritually grounded, you are not attached to any one outcome. No matter what happens, you won't be afraid to see the truth as it really is, you won't hide behind issues you were afraid to face. You know that no matter what occurs, there is a reason and lesson behind it, which makes a positive outcome certain.

Opening Your Heart

Can you intuitively search your lover's heart and truly wish that he have everything he wants and needs to obtain his higher good? Or do you just want him to propose by your next birthday? Can you look into his eyes and wish, with all your heart, that he become all that he can be? Or do you really want him to take the lesser job so he doesn't have to leave town?

These are often not easy questions to answer. In fact, it is what leads a lot of men and women to run away the minute they think they find someone with whom they can really share their life. Even though they truly desire a genuine, committed relationship, they lack the spiritual and psychic skills that would enable them to settle down in one place and build anything solid and strong with an equal partner. Someone gets too close and they immediately start sabotaging the situation by blowing minor imperfections and idiosyncrasies out of proportion. The real work of growth eluded them.

In this case, they were drawn to the illusion of something meaningful. But in the process became so dissociated from their feelings that they became like skilled actors, unconsciously playing whatever part they have been taught from past conditioning to play. Under these circumstances, romance becomes nothing more than a cheap thrill that leads us nowhere.

The problem isn't that we attract a certain type of relationship, but that we ourselves are attracted to it. Many of us get used to the pain. This is why we're often attracted to people who don't want us. We know that they can't commit, yet we feel hurt and surprised later when we find out it's true. Available people confront us with the possibility of real intimacy. They might actually hang around long enough to get to know us and melt our defenses by merely loving us.

All of this stems from the belief that we aren't good enough just the way we are. And, if you think that you are not good enough, you will have a difficult time accepting someone who believes you are. As Groucho Marx said, it's like not wanting to be part of any club that would actually want him as a member.

We may not know consciously how separate and distant we make ourselves, but we experience it physically, emotionally, and in our inability to find happiness. Habitual patterns create distance because we are self-absorbed and unconscious; openness and truth bring us closer together because we are awake and able to look into the depth of our love. Start by intuitively noticing different degrees of closeness and separateness in your body, even in miniscule amounts. Distance feels dry, dull, boring, or lonely. Closeness brings warmth, lightness, joy, and a sense of peace.

In this place between unconsciousness and awareness, we fight ourselves. We want to lie on the couch and watch television all day, but we also want to have a rewarding career. We want to eat junk food, but we also want to be thin. We want to find a close relationship, but we want to hide our fears. By waking up, opening your mind, and blasting down those walls around your heart, you can easily push past this inertia and find what lies within the deeper recesses of the heart. The energy can spill right out of you and into the heart of anyone you choose, taking you to a place beyond these closed boundaries.

A healthy relationship consists of two people, devoted to each other, being true to their path as well as being intimate with each other. We must pay attention to our beloved and spend time realizing their passions and life goals. If you, or he, are being pressured to limit yourself—or worse, to give up on your dreams—in order to placate your partner, it's important to withstand the pressure and continue on your path regardless of any resistance. You must continue to expand. And, he may not. But by staying true to yourself, it won't matter. If the relationship ends, you will understand it was for your higher good. Otherwise, resentment sets in, and eventually resentment turns to anger, and anger to hatred.

We close our hearts only because somewhere along the way the open heart caused embarrassment, humiliation, or pain. Someone didn't care about us, and now we carry that with us into the next relationship. We won't allow ourselves to be vulnerable again. We block intimacy and hide from commitment. We build emotional defenses, the likes of which can sometimes resemble a fortress. We keep blaming someone in the present for something someone else did in the past. Some poor man is paying for what your ex-boyfriend or ex-husband did to you years ago. A disconnect occurred between you and your current partner. You are no longer relating to him, but relating to all the times you felt as though you didn't matter before. At some point, you have to stop and admit that the past is gone and you are willing to let it go.

Personally, I had to uncover my pain and stop worrying about what others thought. I had to let go of stereotypes, categories, and any other misconstrued values and ideas I held. I was forced to explore my motivations. Did I believe that a relationship would fill me up, bring financial security, or keep me from being alone? Did I fear that there wasn't anyone else out there for me? Was I desperate to escape another relationship? Did this all have something to do with leftover childhood memories?

Burn away those barriers. This means we must delve into the core of our being and discover what holds us back and keeps us bound to old beliefs. Only by spending time with yourself and using your intuition to guide you will you be able to heal those wounds. So when he says, "I don't want to talk right now," we're not hurt or distraught with pain. Or if he says, "I need to see a friend tonight instead of spending time with you," you're not paralyzed with jealousy and envy.

Whatever you hide behind, whatever way you have of playing small, open your heart right now and take a look. Admit the things you came up with in the past in order to survive, but that no longer serve you. You are not a little girl, and he is not a little boy. We are adults who attract adults and have adult relationships. If you want to live life in a big way, you must learn to love in a big way.

Get rid of the games you have been playing and the drama you have been creating, and pay homage to the beauty and innocence in others. In this way, you are both healed. Finding our full magnificence allows us to see it in everyone else. Then we all grow more quickly into our destiny and do the most for ourselves and the world. That's because we are most powerful when we no longer find it necessary to exert power over others or the world around us.

In a relationship this means that you are one hundred percent committed, with all the vulnerability and un-certainty of a predestined outcome. You no longer look at the person and wonder if they will be with you next year—there is no next year. You no longer look at the person and wonder if they will take care of you ten years from now—there is no ten years from now. You simply open your heart and allow what will be … to be.

Here and now, we can awaken our hearts to the vast-ness that lies within. It requires an effort, but that's not the same thing as struggle, as you are about to find out. It is about accepting our experiences, letting go of all past teachings that no longer serve us, and living within the moment. Life continues to flow. All you have to do is let go and move into the flow by being present in the moment with a loving heart and a free mind. True love awaits.

The past is over;
it was nothing more than a dream.
The scent no longer lingers on the pillow,
on which you rest your head.
Forget with me, my love.
Forget what never was.

EXERCISE

Hand On Your Heart Meditation

Simply placing your hand on your heart chakra can work wonders. By connecting your physical body to the heart center, you are reminding yourself of who you truly are: a spiritual being that is in the world, but not *of* this world, made in the likeness of pure love.

Every time you feel lost, look into your heart and remember where you're going and why. And feel what you feel in your heart. Breathe into the area. Imagine the space around your heart softening. Now imagine your heart chakra becoming light and spacious. Free.

If you are in a situation where it's hard to put your hand on your heart, another way to do this is to simply take your own pulse. Place your finger on your pulse and feel your heart beating. At the same time, pay attention to the pause between the beats. The beat is life, the pause is death, and when we realize this, we can only love ourselves more.

One of the main ways you access your intuitive self is through your heart. Whenever you are confused or troubled, ask your heart what it has to say. Then acknowledge it and affirm that you will listen to and act on its promptings. In the end, the higher source can only be experienced through the heart.

Tune In to Yourself First

In relationships, as in life, it's quite easy for people to become attached to praise, validation, sex, security, status, and affirmations of their worth. Sentiments such as "You make me feel so good," or "You make me feel so bad," are both forms of attachment, because no one else can make you feel good or bad. In the end, no one can even break your heart—you do that to yourself. It may sound harsh, or cruel, but it is true. As Shakespeare said, "There is nothing either good or bad, but thinking makes it so."

This doesn't mean that we don't support each other, but there comes a point where you should not depend on validation from another person, nor should they depend on that from you. Love is not codependency. Love should be a natural, organic outpouring.

You are naturally attuning to people and situations all the time. From your own internal sense of intuition, you become receptive from every physical perspective, from your partner's tone of voice to his body language, the depth of his breathing, and even the way he moves. A smile, a concerned look, a glance, a nod, all take on significance and meaning.

We tune in to our Sacred Self by saying or hearing things such as "That doesn't sound good," or "It doesn't feel right to me," or "I got a knot in my stomach when you said that." We will know if something doesn't feel right, because we ourselves will feel it in our uneasiness or sensations that run through our body or mind, and can then determine where these feelings are coming from.

Clients come to me all of the time with problems they feel are being caused by their partner. But by tuning in, they come to realize that the issue usually doesn't have anything to do with their partner, but with themselves.

Take Tammy, for instance. She quit a job she didn't like and got married all within a few months' time. Six months later, she felt disappointed and let down. She expected that once she married, everything would be different and her life would change for the better. Now her husband was withdrawing more and more and wasn't making her happy. She wondered if she had made the right decision, and contemplated leaving him. "If I get out of this marriage, maybe everything will be all right again," she said.

But when she entered her sacred space and tuned in to her own feelings and his, she came to understand that she was really looking to him to fill the emptiness she felt inside. She just left a job, and had no direction of her own, no goals whatsoever, and somehow imagined that being married would "fix" everything. Once she got inside of her own heart chakra, she came to the conclusion that there was nothing wrong with her marriage or her husband, but with herself. No matter how much he loved her, he couldn't fill that void within her. She had to do that. And that meant that she couldn't just go to the gym every day, watch television, and cook and clean and feel fulfilled. Tammy stopped seeking sustenance from her partner.

Further investigation into her Sacred Self led her to sign up for a class and start volunteering for a local charity.

Both provided her with a sense that her life had a purpose outside of her marriage. Five years later, she's still married, finished school, and has a job as a registered nurse in the pediatric ward of their local hospital.

Tuning in comes from a relaxed, receptive state motivated by a desire to know, to understand, and to resonate with ourselves and another person. The purpose is to connect, not necessarily with the other person, but with how we feel about what the other person is doing or saying. Then and only then can we get to the heart of the matter.

To become attuned, start by taking a deep breath, release it fully, then relax each of your muscles. Drop back into your body. Center yourself. Focus on each organ as if you were examining it with a flashlight, zoning in on tension, calm, fear, thoughts of judgment.

If you take time on a daily basis to go to your quiet place and meditate, you'll find that you no longer care so much about how someone else is treating you, but how you are treating yourself. Also, take a minute every now and again throughout the day to stop yourself and ask, "What am I feeling right now and why?" It naturally activates the current of awareness that is constantly running through our lives.

Next, do the same with your partner. Take the time once a day to silently tune in to how he is feeling. You can do this while he is present, or by simply visualizing him. Relax and focus on his heart chakra and ask the same question, "What are you feeling right now?"

On a physical level, it doesn't hurt to ask questions, either. "How was your day?" or "What's on your mind?" can be equally as effective. By asking questions and listening intently to the answers, it not only helps you, but helps them to hear more clearly.

The purpose here is connection. And when we stay connected with ourselves and with those we love, we move out of our own way and allow the Universe to guide us.

EXERCISE

Creating a Sacred Space

When you fall in love, you embark on a great adventure. The journey begins by entering into a sacred space within yourself, and there's no better way to find that internally than to find it externally first. All of us deserve to have our own special place to go and be one with our creator. As we meditate and intuitively delve deeper into our soul, our mind naturally starts to quiet down. You then become a witness to the unfolding drama of your life and see it for what it truly is. You effortlessly step out of your own way.

Whether you know it or not, you create sacred space all the time. The last time you decided to take a really special bath, did you light candles? Incense? Or how about an intimate get-together with friends? Did you light the fireplace, along with some candles? Maybe you put on some mood music? Why? Because it creates an energy that fills the room and the people in it. So why not take the same care when we want to do our most important work—the work on ourselves? When it's time to meditate, or journal, or work on our affirmations and visualizations, I think it's extremely important that you create an atmosphere where those ideas can flourish.

Start by finding a place that is all your own. I don't care if it's a closet (although that's not ideal) or a small corner of a room, just make sure it's yours and yours alone. Gather up some items that mean a lot to you, such as figurines, photographs, incense, candles, and mementos that have significance in your life. If you can spread them out and keep them in your special place, great. If not, keep them in a box or basket that you can pull out when the time is right.

The reason for doing this is that it enhances your intuitive abilities. Once you meditate in this space and continue to do so, then the next time you visit, the process will take half the time. You can come to your space and be calm and relaxed almost instantly, as the brain has been triggered to believe that when you are in this place you will actualize your essential nature and make conscious contact with a higher source.

A word about candles when trying to romance your flame. I use different colors for whatever area I am focusing on. For instance, yellow for clarity, green for healing, blue for calming, orange for energy, and purple for intuition. A lot of people choose red for love, but I rarely do.

It's rather aggressive and sometimes overly passionate. If you're not careful, it can push you overboard and create negative energy. So if you're a novice, for any work on love, use pink. It will have the same effects energetically and not be overwhelming.

The one color you can always use, and the one I use most often for everything and anything, including candlelit dinners, is white. White reflects all colors, like a prism, and its purity always leads me in the right direction.

When you sit down in your sacred space for the Sacred Self, light the candle, open your heart chakra, and allow the love and light from the candle to enter. By doing this you will release any negative energy and set the stage for the Universe to fill you with information and healing. Bathe in the grace of the light and let the inner voice of your heart gently guide you to any answers you may need.

Now ask yourself, What brings you pleasure? What have you always wanted to do that you haven't done? What would help you grow as a person? Feel the pulse of your own life.

I remember the first time I took my daughter on an airplane. She was about three at the time and we both sat and listened to the flight attendant give us instructions on what to do in an emergency. She got to the part about oxygen masks popping out of the overhead, and informed us to place the mask on ourselves first, before anyone else, including a child. I thought she was crazy.

As a mother, it was my natural instinct to save my child first. But she said, and it's a good point to remember, "If you haven't helped yourself first, how can you help anyone else?"

If you can't find a sacred space within your home, try venturing outward. We find ourselves from the inside, but sometimes that's easier to do outside. Try one of the following to help you find spiritual communion:

The Ocean: Waves move as your breath. As an added benefit, the negative ions in the air can change your brain waves.

The Forest: Nature surrounds you with its own positive energy of rebirth and regrowth. Allow it to shelter and soothe you.

The Garden: Plant something and watch it grow. It will fill your heart with nourishment. While you're there, hug a tree. The life force it takes for a tree to draw water from the ground is enormous. When you make contact, that energy transfers through your system, cleansing you internally. That's why it feels so good. Besides, the tree appreciates it.

We all need space to be creatively intuitive, yet it requires nothing more than solitude. This is the only time that we can heal both physically and spiritually. Alone. So whether it's a room of your own, a bathtub, a bed, a closet, or standing in front of a waterfall, find that place where your rare, deep, and wide Sacred Self can thrive.

Whatever space you choose, take the time to protect it and bless it. This can be as simple as asking your higher power to remove any negative energy from your space and that it be cleansed and neutralized. Remember, this is your sanctuary, and you are using it to inspire your teachings of higher perceptions. Love it and protect it.

Effort versus Struggle

Ram Tzu writes in *No Way: A Guide for the Spiritually Advanced*, "The more you pursue it, the further away it goes."

All relationships take work. That's because they will push all your buttons, try your faith, challenge your strengths, trigger your weaknesses, mock your values and, at times, leave you flat on the floor at four in the morning looking for something, anything to hold on to. Relationships are constantly evolving. They are not fixed. And no two ways about it, real change is messy.

Effort is a natural part of the process. I mean, even if there is a million dollars on the floor in front of you, you still have to get up off your beautiful behind and pick it up. Effort is a must. But effort is completely different than struggle. Struggling is effort laced with emotion and will always cause upset. It's like trying to paddle your boat up the stream. You can row and row, but in the end you won't get very far. Most likely, the reason you are trying to do this in the first place originated from a preconceived picture of how you want your partner to behave. This has nothing to do with experiencing them as they truly are, and it rarely works.

The next step, which many of us have been taught, would be to "figure things out," or "make" a relationship work. But from a spiritual perspective you can't "make" anything happen. We must stand back from the mind and this prior learning and resonate with spirit and our own intuition. We must revert back to our essential being, or what the Buddhists call the "beginner mind," and realize we are not experiencing our partner as they truly are. From this perspective, we come to understand that we cannot "get" anything, we can merely "let" it happen.

Have you ever tried to convince a cab driver to take you somewhere he doesn't want to go? He says, "No way, lady," or the rough equivalent in another language. Would you honestly stand there determined to convince him otherwise? Meanwhile, cab after cab flies by, but you're stuck there trying to talk someone into taking you where they don't want to go.

We all have done it at one time or another, only to discover that there is a better way to get where we want to go. Sooner or later, we step up and say, as the much attributed quote goes, "I'm not okay, you're not okay, and that's okay!"

If you can allow and just let things happen as they should, then you will stop interfering and finally be on your way! So you see, it's not about *getting* anything, or *getting* anywhere. It's about *letting* it happen. How do we do that? By remembering that if it's not working, it's not meant to. With that one thought, we allow the grace of the Universe to step in and take over. It forces you to stop complaining and finding other people to complain with you. And there are lots of them out there, trust me. You can recognize women who do this—they always seem to look a bit haunted and scurry back and forth a lot, without going far.

I have many clients who fall into relationships—be they healthy or unhealthy, loving or abusive, fulfilling or destructive, functional or highly dysfunctional—just because they want to be in one so badly that the relationship itself ceases to matter. They are in a relationship, after all.

There's nothing spiritual about falling into the wrong relationship with the wrong person for all the wrong reasons. Our sixth sense is the key. The Universe is trying to tell you something. Listen up! By keying into your intuition, you will hear the answer.

So don't allow yourself to slide into that seductive negativity that will convince you that you are right to hold onto something that can burn you, or potentially destroy you, or get you really, really lost. Choosing acceptance over the critical, judgmental darkness allows the light to flood in and will always enable you to see clearly. That's a reason they say love is blind, but it need not be. Open your eyes and choose a deliberate act of personal revolution. Let your most alive Sacred Self rule. It knows where you should go and when, so hold on—you're in for the ride of your life!

EXERCISE

Staying Solid as a Rock

Grounding crystals that you carry with you (or sleep with) keep you centered and connected to your intuitive senses. Whenever you feel you are trying too hard to force a situation into being what you want it to be, or trying to make something happen, simply reach for one and hold it in your hands. Then hold it over your third eye and imagine this unwanted energy flowing out of you and into the crystals. Repeat the following:

Take from me my temptation to control another.
Take from me the games I play.
Teach me to forgive, and not to judge.
I surrender my love.

Obsidian: Because it is volcanic rock, Obsidian is excellent for blocking energy, making it an excellent stone for people who find they tend to pick up other people's negative energy and must work with large groups.

Hematite: This rock stabilizes emotions.

Green Fluorite: Good for balancing and calming the nervous system.

There are so many more stones to choose from that you can investigate, but these are the ones I use most often that work for me. Explore. Whichever ones you choose, remember to cleanse them often in salt water, or by leaving them outside under the moonlight.

You Are Not Here to Fix or Change Anyone

Whenever we find ourselves frustrated, irritated, or becoming manipulative, I guarantee it has something to do with wanting someone, or something, to be different than it is. When we try to mold a person into an image of what we want rather than getting to know and appreciate them as they are, we create separateness, frustration, and a hell of a lot of pain.

When we become less insistent on having things our way, we can lift the monkey off our back and find peace. The issue is not to get someone to be who you want them to be. Real relationship is not about fixing someone, or getting them to fit some picture in our head. Accept your partner as they are. When you do, miracles occur. We change faster when someone is not trying to make us change in the first place! If someone tells you to be nice, and you try to be nice, chances are you are not really being nice—your heart's just not it, and it shows.

Most of us have preconceived ideas of what we think we need. And we want what we want. It's similar to walking around with a picture frame, trying to find the perfect image to fit inside. In reality, we should start with the picture and then frame it. But our fears find us. Self-indulgently, we wonder if this person will stay, or how long they will stay, or if they will meet our needs. We're starting off with, "I can't love you as you are, so please change." It's all about what you're getting, and not at all about what you're giving.

Instead of creating scripts and pictures of how we want a situation to evolve, we must intuitively step into our Sacred Self with complete awareness. When we do, we set limits and respond simply, without throwing the other person out of our heart. We see the whole package, foibles and flaws included, and then decide if we can accept them or not.

For instance, if you date a younger man, you need to give him permission to be young. A client named Jan couldn't understand why her boyfriend, twelve years her junior, didn't want to spend more time at home with her, watching movies and just "chilling." He wasn't interested in chilling. He wanted to go out and have fun, travel more, and always be on the go. Once she consulted her intuition, she came to the conclusion that he was just being who he was: a young man, experiencing as much of life as he could. Who was she to stop him? In some cases, this could work itself out, but in Jan's case, she knew that by trying to "make" the relationship work, she would only be forcing him to be something that he wasn't ready, or equipped, to be. Jan moved on.

If you date a high-powered business executive, it would be highly unfair to suggest that he spend more of his time with you when you know his work takes priority. You can't change how he conducts business, and even if he was willing to do so, he might resent it and, eventually, you. Either way, it's the person who isn't getting what they want who needs to give more and/or move on. Otherwise, all we succeed in doing is trying to control someone else.

Keep an intuitive grasp on your attachments and images of what you feel is "right" for you. Most of the men who fit the image of what I thought I wanted turned out to be quite nasty to me. Those relationships ended horribly. Then someone came along who wasn't exactly what I thought I was looking for, and he turned out to be perfect. Keep open, keep laughing, and keep doing your dance in the center of your own life. Just don't try to change someone or allow them to change you.

If you really believe you can change a man, think again. I'm not talking about making him pick up his underwear off the bathroom floor in the morning, or getting him to finally stop making those annoying slurping sounds when he eats his cereal or (worse) refusing to close his mouth when he chews his food. I'm talking about the big things in life. Like getting him to stop watching Monday night football, or actually believing that some day he could fall in love with you enough to make a lifetime commitment, despite all outward signs to the contrary.

Enlist help. Ask your intuition if you really do feel he actually could or would even be willing to change. Be honest. You cannot inject yourself into the answers. You must be completely open to hear what the Universe tells you.

Guaranteeing You Will Have a Committed Relationship

Women who find themselves in deeply committed relationships have different relationship dynamics. For starters they intuitively shift into a "we" consciousness that virtually promises that they will be with one person and only one person. They also have the following three things in common:

They are committed to being committed. In other words they are certain, without a doubt, that they will have a life partner, and nothing can convince them otherwise.

They do not waste time with dead-end relationships. These are relationships that are destined not to work in the first place: dating a married man, convincing themselves that a man will get over drugs or alcohol, or continuing to date a man exclusively even if he is still seeing other women. They intuitively only sought out and dated someone who was ready for a long-term relationship, because they stayed within their spiritual center.

They love themselves more than they love anyone else. This is not from an egotistical standpoint. They didn't just focus on finding the right man; they focused on becoming the right woman.

Building a connection with another person is a natural part of our existence. We are meant to live in bliss, and this is intricately tied to others. Longing for a lover is an expression of longing to awaken our hearts. But that person does not possess the power to take away or give us happiness and joy. That comes from the spirit within us, and a partner only enhances that within us and within themselves. No one can make you happy, or reject you, or break your heart. Only you can. Understanding this sets you free from the ego. You will no longer hold back or play small, but instead allow your spirit to soar. This is true power, because you will not be tempted to abandon yourself, compromise your ideals, or discount your intuition.

When we stay in the center of our own life, we trust our intuition and allow it to guide us, without worrying about whether it's right or wrong or what others will think. We flow within ourselves. And the more we flow within, the more we flow without.

2

SHINING THE LIGHT ON YOUR DARKNESS

Your task is not to seek for love, but merely to seek and find all the
barriers within yourself that you have built against it.

—RUMI

Spiritually, relationships are mirrors. How you see your-self is how another will see you. How you think of yourself is how they will think of you. If you don't already believe you are capable of a warm, loving relationship, then another person will never be convinced of it either.

Now, here's the thing. If you looked into a mirror and saw something you didn't like, could you honestly blame the mirror? You and I both know by now that no one is perfect. That's why we push each other's buttons—not so we'll run off and hide, but so we'll be forced to face our reflection.

Everyone has a shadow side, especially when it comes to love. When you shine a bright light on yourself, you are going to see things you don't want to see. Our ego distances us through denial or dissociation, but our intu-ition will bust us and show us the truth about the games we play.

Why go there? Because you can't move past these issues until you really see them. When you shine that flashlight on your fears, you will find it is not only easier to forgive yourself, but to forgive anyone who "helped" you become the person you are today.

We are all learning, or we wouldn't be here on this planet today. And it's only through our spiritual perfection that we heal our imperfections. A teacher in India once told me that when you look into muddy water, it's still clear. You may have to wait until the mud settles, but it is still clear.

So I ask you, can it be that the real purpose of a relationship is to bring out all of those imperfections? Well, I hate to break it to you, but, yes it is. It's what makes a romantic relationship so fantastic and at the same time so difficult. Relationships build our character. We are forced to remove the scabs that cover our cuts and bruises and allow the fresh air of spirit to heal them. It's almost like performing psychic surgery on ourselves. Only then can you cut into the emotional and psychological diseases that need to be removed. The way the Universe does this is to send us those who will challenge us and help us nurse ourselves back to health. It's tough work, but then we get to live in a place where the enchantment flourishes and grows.

Relationships are not material, but spiritual, and the part the two people play is all about moving beyond our stuff. And I don't care who you are, we all have stuff. If you just want to be comfortable and not have anyone call you on your phobias and fears, you won't grow. Basically, what you're saying is "Please love me, but don't you dare challenge my BS." That might make you feel better temporarily, but sooner or later, the other person catches on. You can't hide the real you forever. And if you're not willing to grow and evolve, I bet they are. And, once they do so, they usually leave.

You have to show up fully, but that's hard to do when you don't know how to show up for yourself. And, conversely, how you want a man to show up for you will be completely dependent on how you show up for him.

Love is a participatory emotion. I ended up getting the most out of a relationship when I stopped focusing on how he was doing and directed my attention to how I was doing. What was the level of my commitment in the relationship? When I stepped up, miraculously, he did too. When I took the interaction off of him, the relationship unfolded much more constructively. For instance, I'm not gorgeous in the morning, trust me. And neither was he. But love is a decision. Waiting to see if someone else is going to step up is silly. I stepped up. I stopped being nervous about how I looked first thing in the morning, and when I did, I could see he didn't care. He loved me with my eye boogers and all.

In other words, no man can make you feel like a real woman until you feel like one already. You cannot hold yourself separate and demand that they own up to the person you *think* you want to become. Or, for that matter, what you want him to become. When you join a partner just as they are, your approval and unconditional love allows them to shine. And, when they shine, you shine.

From an outside perspective, we want to find someone attractive enough to support, but from a spiritual perspective, we should be looking for someone who supports us in being attractive. I have been told I'm not good enough, but when I realized what that man meant was that I wasn't good enough for *him*, it all made sense.

How can we give a part of us if we're not really sure there's anything there to give? How can we extend our light when we don't really believe we have light in the first place? The light is there. We have simply blocked it. If you think it's not there, you're delusional. We are all one in spirit, and therefore we are deeply equal in spiritual essence, bound by this light, not by our differences. In this psychic womb, we give birth to true love.

All of us have a lot to give. In fact, we have not even scratched the surface of how much infinite potential we all possess. If we are each a wave in the ocean, we cannot be separate from the rest of the ocean. The ocean is within us, and if we intuitively connect with that, we will naturally allow it to cleanse and nourish us, and our relationships. We block that flow when we forget where the wave comes from and what it is attached to. So if your core belief is that you are separate and he is separate and maybe you'll bump into each other, then all you are talking about is sex.

Remember, it's the light coming from the lamp that matters, not the lamp. It's the innocence and grace of knowing this that allows your life and love to move in natural harmony, exactly when they are supposed to. Through meditation and intuitive practice, you defer to the spirit moving within you, so that when the light does shine through you, it will also guide you effortlessly to a higher path. When we step back and allow spirit to lead, miracles occur.

In this place, you don't work on a relationship so much as you allow love to do what love does all by itself. It will simply combine two people's energies in ways that lift their lives up to a place where new ideas, new possibilities, and new opportunities emerge.

Your job is to not hinder the process by remaining in the dark. It's not about the past or the future. It's not about practicality and societal or worldly routines. It is a bold and masterful inquiry into who two people really are and how we might become the people we want to become.

When I first got serious about men, I continually chose ones who wouldn't commit. Subconsciously, I wasn't ready for marriage. I thought I was. I even convinced myself I was, mostly because all of my friends were doing it, and as I approached thirty, I thought I had better get on with it, because my biological clock was ticking louder and louder, to the rhythm of "How old do you want to be when you have children?" But my intuition told me to hold off and wait. And I did.

So, let me ask you, How committed are you? How prepared are you in the deepest recesses of your being to give and receive love in an intimate way? Can you forgive those who could not go past a certain wall of fear when dealing with you? Can you forgive yourself for the ways in which you contributed to, or participated in, their fear?

Hopefully, by asking yourself these questions, you can grow beyond the emotional torture chamber we sometimes place ourselves in and understand what we really need to work on: mutual sharing, and not mutual attack or judgment. Darkness must be exposed before it can be transformed. You don't want to hide your issues.

A client, Angie, came to see me because she planned on leaving her boyfriend. She claimed he "wasn't available for the experience."

I asked Angie to take a minute and meditate. I wanted her to intuitively check in with her Sacred Self and ask, Who exactly isn't available? If she shared what she thought was love from a spiritual and intuitive perspective, then his behavior shouldn't define her relationship. We cannot know true love if we are seeking to make someone act the way we want them to act. She discovered that her emotional stability rested on him being at her beck and call. He wasn't unavailable so much as he was frightened of being smothered. When she released him energetically, he came around on his own.

Intimacy is not something we go out and find, as if you were bargain shopping for a designer outfit or a new pair of shoes. Intimacy has already been created by the Universe and is just waiting for you to try it on. To conquer love is to conquer yourself. Until you see someone's dark side, you won't know who they really are. And, until you see your own darkness, they won't know who you really are. You can run, but you can't hide. Your self-contempt will always catch up with you somewhere down the road.

If you believe that you are an abundant person, and that he is an abundant person, then you will really dance.

And when you forget you are special, and he forgets he is, remind each other that these thoughts are only illusions. Don't try to fix the illusions, nag them, criticize them, or belittle them, but show them what's what by being your abundant self. By permitting your light to shine, you allow others to as well.

How do we do this? By letting go of the past and starting fresh. Everyone's childhood was hard. Everyone has made mistakes because of it. I get it. I have yet to meet anyone who can tell me they had the perfect upbringing. Now you simply have to intuitively reprogram yourself from a subliminal level, by meditating regularly. This moment is all there is. Healing doesn't happen in the past or in the future, only in the here and now. We are not victims unless we choose to be. So whatever someone did to you, learn from it, psychically forgive them, and let it go. Move forward now with me into the dream you were meant to live.

Eckhart Tolle in *The Power of Now* reminds us that when we have a problem we have three choices: leave the situation, change the situation, or accept it completely. Otherwise, it occupies tremendous energy and keeps us from being present.

The Masks We Wear

This is where we all get naked. Truly naked. But, first, let's get your mind out of the gutter, and figure out what this really means.

Meet your Sacred Self. That's who you'll find beneath the mask. The real, naked you. And when you are naked, you let your wounds show. Not so someone can hurt you, but so that they can heal you. If they punish you for your scars, then they are not your partner. If they want to help you heal them, then they are. Otherwise, there is no point.

Coming together is about being our authentic self, while being able to belong and coexist within a partnership. You stop wasting time with desperate scenarios that try to convince somebody that you are someone you are not.

If this feels foreign or uncomfortable, it might be that past traumas and pains you haven't dealt with are causing you to hide your real self. No matter where you are on this path of life, it helps to remember that we all wore a costume or mask of some sort or another at various times. You were a good girl, you were a bad girl, smart, silly, tough, charming...and the list goes on. As a result, we end up navigating through life disguising our true nature. The more we are willing to take off those masks, the more we can create trust, safety, and honesty within ourselves and in a relationship. My fears meet your fears, and nobody runs away. Instead, we turn up the music and dance.

The first step in taking off a mask is to simply realize that you're wearing one in the first place. If, for instance, you are wearing a tough career woman mask, you must first acknowledge that. By agreeing to reveal this mask for what it is, you discover the role that has become ingrained and automatic to your life. By removing this mask, you open up to the deeper exploration of the inner, authentic person you are. Perhaps you have pushed a partner away and made work a priority, for fear that you could lose this persona.

The ego tricks us into making excuses and pushing people away so we can give up responsibility of ourselves. Sometimes we feel the mask belongs to someone who knows what they are talking about, and we start to believe them. But the mask is still a mask, and we fall for that trick in order to deflect our own insecurities.

Our task is to crack through and soften the layers upon layers of personas and masks we have donned to protect us from the false core beliefs that cover our hurts, losses, and loneliness. Become intuitively aware of your masks. Become curious about their purpose, amused by their cleverness, yet always remain aware that masks are simply that: façades. A mask can't love someone; only the warrior behind the mask can.

If you can't take off your mask, it might help if you learned the reason you created it in the first place. We can remove these coverings in a thousand ways, but what helps the most is to know that we can stop showing off and say, "I'm afraid," if you really are. You can finally stop pretending to be someone you're not by recognizing the fear that you've been covering up and hiding from the world. It then becomes your own, and when it does, you can take it off.

My own history with men is so sordid that I'm almost embarrassed to admit it. So, let me just give you the highlights. It has included married men, violent men, con men, immature men, liars, cheaters, the I'm Not Readies, the desperate, the lost, the psychotic, the users, and the losers. I attracted into my life exactly what I thought my masked self deserved at the time. But I thought I could get them to follow my agenda and help them to change. I did not succeed, needless to say. All I accomplished in the process was wasting my time. Once I got into my thirties, I realized that wasn't an option anymore.

So did I stop meeting any of the above types of men? No, I was just getting started! I met them again and again. The difference is that somewhere along the way, I learned that these were the masks these men wore—I could not take them off for them. You think that's an easy realization? It's not. I had to come to the conclusion that yes, these men in masks were out there. But that didn't mean I had to give them my phone number. I wasn't going to let my addiction to the wrong types of men keep me down anymore.

I finally rid myself of the sick, romantic myth that someone was going to come along and unblock me, rescue me, and if they were doing it from behind a façade, so what? Trouble is, I fell in love with the mask and not the man and, when he took it off, I was toast. Then I started telling stories to my friends about it, eliciting sympathy and convincing myself it was the man's fault. If someone falls in love with a mask, they have two choices: lose themselves, or remove the mask along with their own and see what happens, even if it means that they might lose the relationship.

When you drop your front, you invite someone to do the same. Some people won't be able to, because when attention is placed on the genuine person they are, they get scared. They worry that if you see the real them, you won't want them anymore. Do not despair. Remember, you are not falling in love with them, but with the disguise they are wearing. If you want true love, neither one of you can hide the real you.

So be completely honest with yourself. Meditate and delve into your heart and soul. Then ask yourself, Are you really portraying the person you would like to be, or are you wearing a mask that is old and outdated, something you simply forgot to take off as your life progressed?

Also become aware of the masks that other people wear. Spend some time meditating on your man as he really is. Intuitively look at him through your third eye. Are you viewing him as wearing a mask? One that you undoubtedly gave him to wear without even realizing it? You and your partner should be in the relationship because of who you both are *right now*. Not who you will become, or who you once were.

I dreamt I stood in front of my love, a daisy in my hand. I pulled off a petal one at a time. "One for my love, two for my forgiveness, three for my surrender, four for my understanding, five for my truth, six for my commitment, seven for my true self."

No more petals, no more flower. "Do you still want me?" I asked him.

"Yes," he said. "And I shall love you more than before."

Another way to unmask the masked man is to have a conversation with your inner child. When you were young, you didn't have to try to receive impressions, you were just open to their existence. Just pretend that everything has a meaning, and it will. This is one of the easiest ways to distinguish between the voice of your inner self and those that you are just making up in your head.

Another way I connect with the child within me is to simply play. Ask questions and just see what answers come to you, even if it's through a song on the radio, a sign on a billboard, a symbol that comes to you like a butterfly, or a cloud in the sky. Also, pay particular attention to intuitive impressions that enter into your realm of consciousness just as you are about to fall asleep. The veils between the waking world and sleeping world are very thin, and those few seconds or minutes when you aren't certain if you are asleep or awake are mystical and magical. Rational thinking is really hard when you are standing on the cliff of sleep. Take advantage of this non-time and keep a journal by your bed. Record what feelings or thoughts you are having about the man you are with, the relationship, and your future together.

Or you can do this first thing in the morning, while you are still lingering in the dream state, but slightly awake. Ask your inner self about your partner. However you choose to do it, do it with the intention that any information you receive is not only for your higher good, but for his. Is there anything that you haven't seen about this man? Anything you are choosing to ignore because you feel it would be better in the long run, when you know it isn't? Is there anything you should focus on to find out more about a certain habit or quirk he might have that is bigger than you are choosing to believe it is?

Remember, if you feel calm and clear about the interpretations you receive from your intuitive center, then they are true. Tune into the real person. When you do, you will likely see the truth about them and not just the mask you were hoping to see.

Tell Me Your Story, and I'll Tell You Mine

Your story, the story you have been telling yourself over and over again, defines who you are and, therefore, every relationship you've ever been in.

They are the stories that say things like: *be careful, don't get too close*; *you can't trust anyone*; *they might be using you*; *who needs or even wants love?*; *I am really not looking for that*. These are the stories we've been telling ourselves since we were children. It's how we protected ourselves then, and how we protect ourselves now.

One client, Sharon, said that she had to continually work at her relationship and always felt as if she was the one that always had to "give." By using her intuition and delving deeper, we discovered that this stemmed from her childhood. Her mother never seemed to give Sharon the attention and love she longed for as a child. Sharon made up for it by finding herself in relationships where she was forced to love the other person more.

Sharon overcompensated by giving her partner money when he needed it and time when she didn't have it. She bought him too many thoughtful gifts, faked understanding his problems, and acted charming when she didn't feel like it. She repeatedly found herself asking her partner if he was all right. She wanted to keep this man no matter what. She continually found herself in these situations because she started believing her own stories, stories that she invented to protect her false self. The one that told her she was incompetent, inadequate, and unlovable.

Our fears come from the stories we have been repeating to ourselves for so long that we actually buy into them. When it comes to love, we may have experienced a horrific event, had an emotional response, and then created a story to explain it or alleviate our pain. Pretty soon the story takes on a life of its own. I remember reading an article where they interviewed Jack Kerouac and asked him about his book *On the Road*. The reporter asked him if the events really did happen and were, indeed, true. Jack Kerouac responded that they were true, even if they never happened.

We also make up stories based on how our parents, teachers, or other influential people treated us. After awhile, we develop a knee jerk reaction, as if they are absolute truths, rather than ideas planted in our minds. Pretty soon these "truths" become the filter through which we interpret and react to people. *I've always been abandoned* turns into situations where we'll make sure we'll be abandoned.

On a spiritual path, we must leave these stories behind. Intuitively, become aware of when you're not feeling your best or become upset with someone else. How much of that is a story you've been telling yourself? *I'm not good enough for this person; there must be something wrong with me; I can't have a lasting relationship; he'll never stay with me,* and so on. How much of the core belief of these statements are you attracting as a self-fulfilling prophecy?

If you believe that someone else can't love you, you'll keep looking so long that you'll eventually find evidence to support that thought. For instance, if you feel you must constantly protect yourself from getting hurt, you're going to get hurt. These thoughts create so much uncertainty that you'll find problems even when they're not there.

The ego believes these stories to be true, but you don't have to. You can face them squarely and say to yourself, "You know what, that's all a lie. My parents weren't really mean, I did learn how to love, and not every guy out there is a jerk!"

Now I admit that some of us do have deep psychological disorders, in which case one should seek counseling or professional help. Some traumas are too much to work through on your lonesome. But most of us are just attached to the pain. We free ourselves by bringing awareness to the moment and making peace with the past. Notice the sensations in your body or changes in your energy level when you tell yourself a story. Open up your heart and bring yourself back to now. Then stay there.

In the end, the story of your relationship should write itself. All you are supposed to do is take dictation.

Hidden Fears Over Commitment

Fear of commitment is synonymous with the fear of death. For if you are deeply connected with another person, then, by definition, you have to blast down the walls that surround you and surrender to them. Not in the respect that it's the end of who you are as a person, but in the sense that it's the birth of a new self—one that can do things and be someone you could never have imagined before.

It's funny, because even if we don't particularly like who we are, we will always find it difficult to see that image of self die and give birth to something better. And, if you actually never want to change, then the answer is to never fall in love.

I meet women all the time who say they want love but in fact are doing everything in their power to push it away. The ego wants us to remain separate—this is how it thrives. Even if we aren't happy, the status quo is what we know and where we are comfortable. It's easy to get stuck in that rut.

Surrendering is not the loss of power, of putting down our swords so we can't fight back anymore. Surrendering is actually gaining everything, including your own power, because in the end you are not surrendering to another person but to the higher source within you. You are surrendering to the Sacred Self that lies in the center of your being.

If we continually use our intuition to keep our pulse on our inner world, we will hear the song that is ours alone. Then when two people bring their own voices and inner music together, they create harmony, not discord. The notes are divine, the lyrics ancient and mystical. The sound is so magical it cleanses your heart, clears your mind, and transforms your life.

Let's take Susan. She dated a man for three years. Every time she brought up marriage, he became more and more distant. Susan let it go, not wanting to push him. But after a while, she got fed up and broke up with him. Unfortunately, that's not the worst part. Less than six months later, a girlfriend informed her that her ex-boyfriend was engaged. Engaged! And here he kept telling Susan he never wanted to get married! Susan was beside herself and didn't know what to do. What did she do wrong? Really, if she was all that horrible, why was he with her in the first place?

When I worked with Susan, I asked her to check in with her own intuition and tell herself the truth. I sensed that the real issue wasn't about his commitment and more about how committed she was. The majority of women I know who are in committed relationships, whether that included marriage or not, insisted on it. They tapped into their intuition to discover if this was the right man for them. They visualized the outcome and used their own natural, intuitive abilities to broach the subject. Did it ever backfire? Yes, once or twice it did. The difference is that they didn't waste their time. They simply got over it, and moved on.

Essentially, these women didn't get hung up by lust, or put commitment before compatibility, or ignore red flags that made them realize that the relationship wasn't going to work in the first place. They picked what they thought was the right man, but if he wasn't willing to commit, they chalked it up to experience and moved on. They believed, wholeheartedly, that the right one would come along.

Susan brought up the subject with her boyfriend and when he didn't respond positively, she assumed that he would come around and that she shouldn't pressure him. She ignored the intuitive hits that told her that if he wasn't interested by now that he wasn't going to be. And when she looked back, she agreed that she had psychically picked up on these signs but ignored them.

Another thing that prevents some people from committing in any way, shape, or form is an addiction to the attraction phase. They think they want a committed relationship, but the minute someone opens their heart, they close theirs. These people usually have nothing to give in a relationship but will come off as if they're offering the world. They are so disconnected from their own feelings that they have become highly skilled performers, unconsciously playing out the part of someone who wants love and romance, and yet has no idea what that really entails. They get through the romance phase and finally see the real person underneath, and then run like hell. Then they start the process all over again with someone new. We know they are out there. We see them coming. Still, if we weren't looking for a cheap thrill, would we have been so open to the lie?

Where we shut out someone else is where we shut out ourselves. Only through our intuition can we remain cognizant of who and what is really going on. Shutting down doesn't work; piercing the barriers with our psychic abilities does.

First and foremost, we commit to ourselves and then remain true to that on a day-to-day basis by intuitively checking on what we, and our partner, are really doing. One way I do this is to picture both of us surrounded by a bubble of pink light. Then I ask, and keep asking, until I hear a truthful answer.

If you'd like to be in a committed relationship, the first thing I'd like you to do before moving forward is to make a commitment to making a commitment. If you're having a hard time, here's some medicine guaranteed to cure you.

> PRESCRIPTION FOR COMMITMENT MEDICINE
> I, _____, am ready to own
> being in a loving, committed relationship. I deserve
> that because I am PERFECT EXACTLY THE WAY
> I AM!

Take twice daily until you feel you are healed.

Ms. Overly Independent

Considering my parents were immigrants, and we had a bit of a cultural clash going on, I would still say I had a pretty normal upbringing. My father had a career in which he did quite well and provided for the family, and my mother was a housewife. It seemed, however, that as the only girl in the family, the men were the ones doing all the important things in life, while my mother had no choice but to take the back seat. After all, how important could it be to cook and clean and do the laundry? Granted, I now see things quite differently—a mother's role is probably one of the hardest ones there is—but I certainly didn't get it at the time.

Consequently, I did what a lot of young women did at that time and unconsciously came to the conclusion that if I wanted to make a difference in the world, if I wanted to matter and live a life of glamour and meaning, I would have to turn into my father. And that I did. I focused completely upon my career. I was determined to remain strong and fiercely independent. And during the process, I built a wall around my heart that enabled me to keep my emotions at bay. After all, becoming emotional would never serve me in achieving my goals.

I pushed aside relationships that would distract me from my task of becoming the man I supposedly wanted to marry so I wouldn't be forced to marry him. I equated power with money and success. But spiritually, real power has nothing to do with material abundance and everything to do with emotional expansiveness. Men admired me for my success and even loved me for it, but it wasn't the kind of love that wrapped its arms around me on a cold winter night and kept me warm. All it did was leave me cold.

Unbeknownst to me, I had become overly independent. When I met men who were interested in a permanent relationship, I felt so trapped and claustrophobic that I ran like hell. I wanted out so badly that I made certain that the relationship ended. Then I wondered why it hadn't worked out! On top of that, I blamed the men in my life for my condition. I projected my own issues onto them and claimed they were the ones who weren't available, instead of facing up to the fact that I didn't want a commitment in the first place.

It took me a long time to intuitively understand that I purposely picked men who were not going to commit, and if they did, I ambushed the situation. Through meditation and my own intuition, I began to understand that plants can't thrive without water, and humans can't thrive without love.

I had a client named Diana in a similar situation. In her thirties, Diana was a dynamic young woman with a successful career as an artist. She was attractive, with an active social life and lots of friends, yet somehow couldn't manage to sustain a relationship that lasted more than a few months. She either attracted men who had no intentions of making a commitment, or if they did, she found something terribly wrong with them and ended it. In a matter of a few years, she had been involved with dozens of men.

Through her intuition, we discovered that she had con-
flicted feelings about men to begin with. She claimed she
wanted a long-term love, but until she was willing to face
the facts about herself and the reasons she denied intimacy, we could not move forward.

Once Diana reached a clear, calm, meditative state, I
asked her to breathe in the following questions to see if any
of them might help free her from her emotional bondage:

- Are you afraid of rejection?
- Are you afraid of being hurt again?
- Are you afraid of closeness?
- Are you afraid you aren't attractive or smart
  enough to compete with other women out there?
- Are you afraid of having children and a family?
- Are you afraid that a relationship would take away
  from your career, or other interests?

Although there were no easy answers to the questions,
Diana moved through them one by one to discover why
she resisted having a long-term relationship. Once she
did, she understood that after years of dating, failed relationships, and countless disappointments, she had closed
down and become defensive. Intuitively, we had to open
her up again to being vulnerable. By touching base with
her heart chakra, she realized that when she did meet men
who seemed interested, she wouldn't call them back. Without realizing it, she distanced herself from those who could

potentially love her in order to feel safe and secure by remaining angry and afraid.

Part of the process of falling in love is to work through any of the residual feelings we have about men who hurt or betrayed us. We must heal the aggression and anger that stops a relationship before it even begins. As long as we keep ourselves down, we will find partners who agree with that and not allow us to shine with our own magnificence. Once we become women who can welcome a man who won't hold us back but lift us up in all our glory, those men will appear.

Signs of Over-Independence

- You would rather date a guy who was really hot and unavailable than one who is less exciting, but interested in something more permanent.

- You not only have a hard time committing to men, but to girlfriends, work, a class, etc.

- Being in a committed relationship has never been a priority.

- You are continually attracting and dating unavailable men.

- You have been in a relationship with a man you wanted to commit to you, but the minute he did, you declined.

- You hold on to abandonment issues you faced in past relationships.

- You go long periods of time without dating because you feel you're better off alone than being in a relationship.

If you answered yes to even one or two of the above, then you might be commitment phobic and should intuitively relinquish those parts of yourself that oppose forming a sacred bond. It does not take strength to build a wall around our hearts—it takes denial. If we cannot honor our own feelings, no one else can honor them. Internal strength is all that matters in the end, and when we remember this, it is no longer about a man holding us back or making us less than we are or keeping us from our dreams, it's about realizing that we are the only one doing that to ourselves.

We avoid love because it might make us less powerful, but in the end love is all the power there is. On the outer level we may not see that, but on the inner level it is very real, because inwardly love reminds us of the work we still have to do on ourselves. Relationships foster the strength within us, not destroy it. Ask for the circumstances and the person that will make strength and growth possible. Don't ask, and you'll continue to hide from your own glory. Until you embrace the light, you remain effectively in the dark.

EXERCISE

Write from the Heart

Disassociating from your feelings will only cause you to act them out again. Writing down your resistances to what you claim you want is one way you can clear such negativities from your energy field.

Breathe in light and move it upward through your chakras until you reach your throat, the center of your ability to speak and communicate truthfully. (See Chapter Four for more on chakras.) Now describe aloud and in writing what it felt like to be rejected or disappointed by men in your dating life. Have you been betrayed by men who have broken up with you? Did anyone cheat on you, or tell you lies?

Did something happen in your childhood that would cause you to keep a distance from men? Why?

Describe what it was like to turn down a man that was completely into you. Did it make you feel strong and powerful?

More questions will come up as you move through the exercise. Allow them to enter your mind and answer them as truthfully as you can.

When you feel you have completed the exercise, review your notes and process the feelings through meditation. Contemplate your truthful answers without judgment. Then take the piece of paper outside and burn it. Let the ashes go back to the earth and the sky and be rid of those hang-ups once and for all.

Now move your awareness to your third eye chakra, in the middle of your forehead. Take a minute to visualize your future. Imagine what it would be like to live a life of joy and bliss with a significant other. This person loves and adores you, and you love and adore him. Allow your senses to bathe in the emotional security and devotion. How does it feel to you? Is it exciting, freeing? Only see it that way, and you will call into your life exactly what you desire.

Patterns That Plague Us

Relationships will always tempt us to fall into our most neurotic patterns. And guess what? Patterns don't lie. They don't. If an event repeats itself, there's a reason. A pattern is a combination of your thoughts, your emotions and, consequently, your actions. Sometimes patterns can be effective, just as habits can, but that's not what we're concerned about here. We're interested in the ones that mess us up, such as getting into the wrong relationships with the wrong men.

One of the patterns I kept repeating over and over again when I first started seriously dating was that I, like a lot of women, kept picking men who weren't available. It doesn't matter how many affirmations or visualizations I did, nothing changed until I intuitively connected to my inner self and asked what was stopping me from finding a mate. The answer I received at the time was that I had a deep-seated negative belief and fear of marriage that I wasn't addressing. I could do all the meditation I wanted, but until I addressed this issue, nothing was going to change.

Instead of forming my own beliefs and values based on experience and observations, I bought into what I had been taught. I began operating under a litany of rules I didn't even make up. When I did this, I found myself drifting farther and farther away from my true nature. These beliefs are the ones we have to intuitively excavate, mine out of our minds, and destroy.

The problems with patterns? They run pretty damn deep. And for the most part, I've discovered that the majority of women I encounter are already aware of their bad behavior; they just don't necessarily want to do anything about it. So make up your mind that you do want to change and you can probably solve the problem yourself. Unconscious beliefs only remain unconscious until you become conscious of them.

As with all types of limiting beliefs, these often start when we are quite young. Think about how your parents and siblings molded your views on relationships. Did you have a brother who bullied you, or a father who was virtually absent from your life? Also go back to past relationships that may have left you scarred. It could be that a fear of intimacy stems from the bad breakup you had with your very first love.

One way to discover where and how this pattern originated is to make a list of all the men you have had a relationship with. I'm not talking about the guy you had dinner with twice and sex with once and then never saw again. I mean real Relationships. Then take a clear, cleansing breath and relax into a meditative state. Now next to each man's name, quickly—and I mean quickly, as you want your intuition to work for you and not the logical mind that can make excuses and get in the way—list their most negative qualities. One or two words only. Forget the positive, just the negative.

If you do this honestly, I bet that you will see a few words that keep coming up over and over again. Once you've completed the exercise, you'll be able to identify the pattern that you are dragging from one relationship to the next. Again, do not trust your logical mind, as it has a tendency to want to keep you stuck in your old ways. And you, my dear, are no longer willing to do that anymore. You're a changed woman, remember? You found a man, and now you want to make sure he's the right man for you. You want to move forward, not backward or, worse, down the same old rut.

Now comes the hard part: You have to stop and see where you compromise yourself in order to accommodate these traits. This exercise may be tough, but it's the only way to stop sabotaging your heart's desires. Often, it's just the slightest shift in your attention. You acknowledge what you do wrong and then you believe you don't have to continue in the same vein.

Listen, if you empty an old bottle of wine into a new bottle, you still have old wine. You can dress differently and take on a new attitude, but six months later you will still wonder why Mr. Potentially Wonderful turned out to be Mr. He's Just Okay. Can it be that simple? Hell yes.

Our subconscious mind is repeating a pattern in order to give us the chance to fix it, not so it can torture us to death. It's much easier to change before things get unbearable. Otherwise, eventually you will get so sick and tired that you actually get physically sick and tired. The Taoists call this a "kriya," which means a spiritual tantrum, more or less, that will force us to make a change, even if we don't want to.

The subconscious mind is trying to get us to face up to something that is causing discomfort, and sometimes it takes a slap in the face to accomplish this. As someone who's been mentally slapped pretty darned hard at times in my life, I can personally attest to this.

We women are masters of programming our minds with negativity. Without thinking about it, we attack ourselves with thoughts that can sound pretty simple: *I'm having a bad hair day* or *I don't like my figure/my clothes/my relationship/my job/my family*... the list goes on and on. We criticize out of habit and program our mind with beliefs that our life is less than perfect. What we forget is that we are so powerful that we simply create more of the same by focusing on these ideas.

The subconscious hears you and works hard to get you to change, so much so that it never goes to sleep. It works all through the night, even in your dreams. *Especially* in your dreams. I'm not even really sure why it's called the subconscious mind, since it seems to have so much more power than we give it credit for. It's responsible for everything that happens to us in our conscious world. It knows when to make us sick, well, happy, mad, sad, or glad. And the only way to comprehend the manipulative hold it has over us is to delve inside our intuitive mind. It knows where the subconscious lives and until you find it, you can't reprogram it.

Subconscious beliefs are those that are so deeply rooted that we may or may not recognize them in our daily lives. I have a client who truly believes she must act as a different person in order for the relationship with the man she lives with to survive. These are core beliefs, made up from our internal belief systems, that manifest outwardly, like it or not. In the case of this client, her intuitiveness told her that it was her fear of abandonment, which came about when her parents died when she was a young girl, that made her overcompensate in her adult life.

These beliefs stem from a number of different sources. One is our family and what we were taught to believe was right and wrong. The second is the impressions we pick up in life and then don't let go of as we mature and grow. This can be as straightforward as, *My last few relationships didn't work out*, which then translates into *I'm never going to have a lasting relationship with any man*. Ambiguous childhood beliefs can sneak in here as well. *My parents and other people I know had marriages that ended in divorce*, can turn into *Why get married if it's only going to end in a divorce anyway?*

We accumulate these limiting beliefs by not examining our lives carefully and regularly. What makes us tick is what we experience on a day-to-day basis. But how we handle day-to-day living is by accessing information we gathered from a past that is long gone. You may never have had a fear of intimacy until you broke up with your first love. Every experience we have leaves behind a mark, good or bad. If we don't examine these responses, fears, and beliefs, then we carry those thoughts with us for the rest of our lives. Unconsciously, we shape the present, and therefore the future, in negative ways, until we recognize these beliefs for what they truly are and move beyond them.

It may be painful, but in the long run it's for the best. Changing negative patterns will then enable us to live more freely in the present. What you repress, and what you don't, will ultimately determine the success of your relationship. What time doesn't heal, it will reveal. Everything is a lesson.

Repeat after me: "I see my dysfunctional pattern and I choose to end it now."

EXERCISE

Clearing Meditation

We're going to have to talk about meditation, because we always have to talk about meditation. It is the quickest and most effective way I know to increase your psychic and spiritual skills. Not only that, but in so doing, you will manifest what you want into your life, effortlessly. Prayer can also produce the same effects, or any other form of meditation, such as chanting, deep breathing, trance dancing, or a million and one other methods designed to calm the mind and the nervous system. Pick the one best suited to you, and just do it. Consistency and dedication to your higher intent is imperative. Then you are ready to meet your Sacred Self and become more physically, mentally, and emotionally balanced.

Meditation is simply the art of quieting the mind. It is a learned skill and sometimes not easy to do. Your mind can be like a bull in a china shop if you let it. It can be your worst enemy or your best friend, especially when it comes to relationships, because this is where we are most vulnerable. So hold your mind still, or as still as you can, focusing on one thing, a mantra, a phrase, your breath, for as long as you can. What you are doing is breaking a vibrational pattern, which opens our awareness and allows spirit to commune with us.

Your objective is to enter into a light trance, somewhere between partially awake and partially asleep, that place where you are standing on the edge of sleep and are aware of your present surroundings but are no longer concerned with them. You enter into a divinely peaceful consciousness.

I use several meditation techniques, but this is one of my favorites. Yogis (devoted practitioners of yoga) often use this particular meditation, as it calms and quiets the mind effectively and quickly. It uses what I call alternate nostril breathing.

We all breathe, and hopefully you are doing it right now, but rarely do we breathe evenly through both of our nostrils. One of the purposes of meditation is to balance the right and left hemispheres of the brain, and nothing does this more effectively than breathing equal amounts of air into both.

First close your right nostril with your right thumb, and breathe out through the left nostril. Release as much air as you possibly can. Now slowly breathe in through your left nostril. Step two is to close the left nostril with your left thumb and then remove your right thumb from the right nostril. Breathe out through your right nostril, completely emptying your lungs. Now inhale through the right nostril. Alternate nostrils again and close off the right nostril with the thumb and breathe out through the left, just as you did in the beginning. Continue alternating nostrils in this manner.

It sounds more complicated than it is, but once you have done it a few times, it becomes almost a dance that moves in sync with the breathing. When you complete several alternations, you can stop. Then take three cleaning breaths through both nostrils. You will find that you are in a much more optimal state for receiving intuitive insights.

To get in touch with any limiting beliefs and negative thought patterns, ask yourself several questions that you had in mind before you began the meditation process. The first time I did this I simply asked, "What behavior am I continuing to repeat that is hindering my love life?" Boy, did I get an earful. The answer I received was about my patience and temper. And that led me to discover that, on some level, I really thought I didn't *deserve* to be happy and have it all.

A good place to start, I'd say! By discovering these hang-ups and working to get past them, I can now honestly say I have a happy, healthy relationship, not only with myself, but with my perfect man.

Releasing Repression

Carl Jung said, "When an inner situation is not made conscious, it appears outside as fate."

Sometimes eliminating negative beliefs can be as simple as recognizing them. By shining light on a shadow, the darkness itself disappears. It cannot sustain itself when you are aware of it. As with any bad habit, half the battle is acknowledging that you have a problem. The second half is to replace those negative thoughts with new ones.

You can break down potential obstacles by rewriting what you think and feel. Take out a piece of paper and write down the following:

My partner makes me feel
_____ *(upset, resentful)*
because he doesn't _____
(listen to me, respect me, love me). It reminds me
of what happened _____
(last month, week, year, whenever) with

_____.

Not only does this unblock you on a physical level, but on a deeper psychic level. We are always channeling energy, drawing to us what we want and need, especially in a relationship. But if we're unaware of our deep patterns, we block the light from shining through in other areas as well. Your intuitive abilities come from being clear enough to receive information. Keeping ourselves out of the flow of energy ensures that we are polluting the information we receive from a higher source with our own lower-level thinking. Clarity in your life will help you on all levels.

EXERCISE

The Three-Dimensional Vision Board

When the DVD *The Secret* became so popular in 2005, most people who watched it began creating a vision board. They mastered the technique by creating what most likely resembled a collage, similar to the kind we made in school, except of course the images reflected their dreams, hopes, and wishes. Ask most of those people where their vision boards are today and they either won't be able to tell you, or they'll say they are hidden away somewhere, such as in the closet. Not a good idea.

The most important things about your vision board is that it be kept fresh and visible. Put it where you'll see it every day in order to keep your subconscious inspired. As soon as you notice that your board is no longer catching your eye, it's time to sit down and update it. But the next time you do, consider exploring some other options.

There are now vision boards that you can create on your computer and then use as a slide show, wallpaper, screensaver, or have pop onto your screen every hour or so. The obvious advantage of this approach is that you will see your vision board all day long as you work, without any extra effort. I spend the majority of my day in front of a computer and this approach works best for me. It's not as static as a physical board, and I can easily update the images to keep them fresh and inspiring. You can even add a soundtrack, which will produce an even greater impact on your subconscious mind.

Destroy the walls that surround your heart.
Behind them, you will discover,
An enchanted land,
A healed and holy place,
Where you will no longer be held back.
Where you will no longer waste your life.
For all that is broken shall be repaired.
And you become, again, the person you
were meant to be.

Whichever method you choose, make sure that you are including a piece of each puzzle that contributes to your dream. Historically, magazines were the best source for photos, and now online sites are available with an unlimited supply of images. (Hint: try the "image" function of Google if you haven't yet.) You'll also want to pull out your business card collection, and other special items such as favorite quotes and inspiring articles. You don't have to spend money to do this, if you get creative.

The more senses you bring to your vision, the more you invoke your intuitive abilities to manifest them into reality. Stay on course. Distractions become easier to notice when you compare your life to your living vision board. Foster that relationship, and a direct path to your dream will be clear.

The most powerful visioning processes are ones that engage all the senses and are used on a regular basis. I found working with one on my computer a complete immersion experience and so much fun that I want to work with it nearly every day. And that would be the point.

Shining Your Light

The walls around your heart are made of darkness. Even if we don't do it physically with words, people telepathically hear what we are not saying. The toxins we build up inside of us get sent through the airways. Whether we mean them to or not, others can feel this negative energy. I remember dating a man and trying really, really hard not to lean on him or make him feel pressured in any way to see that we were meant to be together. He broke up with me six months later, because he needed his "space." I stated in no uncertain terms that I had been really good about not coming on too strong. I didn't understand. He said he couldn't explain it, that he just *felt* it. He felt me trying to make him commit.

Sometimes shining light on a situation is as easy as asking for it. Go into a meditative state. Think about all of the psychic energy you can channel into your life. It flows through you all the time, and, by becoming aware of it, you can use it to shine light on you, and through you, to help you receive any information you may need. It's quite literally illuminating.

Sit, or stand, still. Now imagine a cord going from the top of your head up into the Universe. Pull down thick, white energy from the cord and fill your body with it as you breathe. Imagine your body glowing from the inside out with this beautiful, illuminated light. Know that this light comes from the Universal Source and is within you to serve only your highest good. Spend as much time as you like in this space and, when you are ready, begin to focus on any area in your life that you would like to see filled with light. Surround it, own it, experience it and all the feelings that go with it. And when you do, you'll become a different person. One that is lighter than air.

There is a big difference between romance and love. When the romance dies down, then and only then, can true love come to light.

EXERCISE

Things That Will Help Your Light Shine

As William Blake said, "If the doors of perception were cleansed, everything would appear to man as it is: infinite." Think of the following as washing the windows to your soul.

Spend time with the very old or the very young. If you have grandparents, this is a great time to reconnect and bond. Most elderly people are full of wonderful life lessons. Not only that, but whether you're conscious of it or not, they force you to face your own mortality. You will be reminded that taking risks is a good thing, if done correctly, and that when all is said and done, loving and being loved is all that matters most in life. Likewise, spending time with young children will open your heart to the spontaneity and joy in life. Children rarely understand judgment, and love unconditionally. Always worth being reminded of.

Clean house. Getting rid of your junk clears the energy for new things to come into your life, especially a relationship. Also, when you dump your past, you lose attachments that are there because we just didn't take the time to examine them and toss them in the trash where they belong.

Visualize happiness. You can change your mind, in every single moment of every single day. Connect with your intuitive side by opening yourself up and seeing yourself

One cold winter night, I said, "It's been so dark, I couldn't see. I am so happy you finally came. What took you so long?"

And he said, "It was so dark, remember? You couldn't see. I've been here all along."

happy and free and in love. Reawaken the center of you that longs to attract that. Being conscious of what you want to achieve each day makes it more likely to happen, especially when you feel your relationship is "being tested." You can and will get through it if you believe you can. As Henry Ford said, "Whether you believe you can do a thing or not, you are right."

3

RELINQUISHING FEARS

Gamble everything for love ...
Half-heartedness doesn't reach into majesty.

—RUMI

et's say you're at a party with your man and he meets a beautiful woman and starts having a conversation with her. Now you can go off in the corner and seethe, act mad, cross your arms and sulk. You say things to yourself like, "How dare he do this?" Especially him, because he already knows all of your issues, and he should know better!

Meanwhile, your blood is starting to boil, because well, look at him over there acting...oh God, happy. How could he?! Then when he finally does come back to your side, you can't even look at him, let alone speak to him. You're mad. You're also full of fear.

Another way to approach this same scenario is to take a step back, close your eyes and take a deep breath. You zone into your inner core and intuitively ask yourself what's really going on. You take another deep breath and suddenly you realize that the answer is...nothing. Nothing is *really* going on. There's nothing to be afraid of. He's having a good time speaking to a nice lady. Why shouldn't he? He's allowed. Hopefully, by continuing to tap into your psychic self, you have figured out that it's not a personal affront to you. You can go and have a good time as well.

Once you remember that love is infinite, that there is no beginning and end, then it doesn't matter what he's doing. And the funny thing is that once he sees you having fun, chatting it up with all the other guys in the room, he'll probably be all over you.

Just remember that love is not a prison or a trap. One of the worst things I hear women say is that they "caught" a man. How do you catch someone? Visions of a hook or a net come to mind, and that just can't be right. We are not on this earth to manipulate anyone. And even if you don't admit that's what's going on, the "prey" will telepathically pick up on it sooner or later.

It takes courage to face your fears, but when you connect with your inner guidance system, your intuition, you will find all of the courage you need. Gerald Jampolsky, MD, wrote in his book *Teach Only Love*, "There are only two emotions: love, our natural inheritance, and fear, an invention of our minds which is illusory. Each instant of the day we choose between these two, and our choice determines the kind of day we have and how we will perceive the world."

Remember, we're all trying to wake up. When a painful situation arises, it means we're holding onto the illusion of separateness. We can't get past the walls in front of our personalities to see the soul of who we are. When we lift the veil, love always returns.

Fear originates from a loss of control. But this is where we must remember that the inspiration and direction we receive from our intuition will always lead us to our higher good. All we have to do is stay true to ourselves, which means that we live with integrity even when it hurts. We may want inner peace, but we are afraid to surrender. We may want a true love, but we are afraid to face rejection or loss. We may want intimacy, but we don't want to give up doing things our way. We must crack the boundaries of these limitations, and the only way to do this is to face our fears.

The process begins by opening up to feeling everything inside. And I mean *everything*. This does not mean we are without discipline or good judgment; what it does mean is that we fear nothing that is intuitively natural. In other words, if what we are being guided to do is easy, it's usually right.

I know that in some relationships in the past, I actually set that person up to leave. And, believe me, I've also had men who were already trying to push me away before I stepped out the door. Sometimes we just cut off love, because we are afraid, and then we feel. The relationship disintegrates into a vat of fear. But wouldn't it be nice to have access to a more sacred way of dealing with this drama? Maybe write a sweeter, more illuminated, ending? You can. It begins by owning the truth.

Even if you see the light of infinite possibilities, you cannot make someone stay. You cannot make them love you. If they make a choice (or you make one) to walk away, then that is to be respected. Just remember that the physical aspect ends, but the spiritual continues. To forgive is divine.

Only then can you fully understand that they are opening you up to a lesson you needed to learn. One that will eventually guide you to greater love, designed for your greater good. Every love builds on the love that came before.

In all honesty, a relationship never rests. It continues to grow and evolve, hopefully into a much deeper place than you ever imagined. But what keeps it going is the fact that you are both fascinated with each other. And the way you stay fascinated is to keep becoming more of who you are. If a man is continually working to keep his woman, always feeling he has to figure out the mystery, he'll never go anywhere. Why? Because this is enchantment. A man who knows that a woman wants him but doesn't *need* him in her life will forever be driven to please her by showing her that he is the only one for her.

When we are completely and utterly free of fear, then there is no holding back. We can drop the armor and tear down the walls and come together with nothing to hide. We bare our souls and let the love flow, without trying, without worrying about our own agenda. Conquering fear is the beginning of true wisdom.

Fear versus Intuition

Taking a step into unfamiliar territory is bound to make anyone uncomfortable. In relationships, when we move from one level to another, we enter the unknown. It's scary. It may be a position you have never been in before, such as marriage, or it could be that you have been there before and are afraid to do it again. You can feel elated and euphoric and fearful all at the same time. That's because you have no idea how it may, or may not, work out. It helps to remember that everyone feels anxious and afraid, and your partner probably does too. The important thing is to not allow this fear to stop you from living your life to the fullest.

One of the questions clients most often ask me is "How can I understand the difference between my intuition and my fear?"

It's a good question, because sometimes fear serves a purpose and keeps us out of danger. But there's a way to distinguish the difference. When I first decided to move in with a man, I felt anxious and fearful and even a bit paranoid. But when I intuitively touched base with my true feelings, I was beside myself with joy. These emotions did not make me feel down and depressed. This time I felt as if everything was falling into place easily and effortlessly. It *felt* right.

If moving in had been a constant struggle, or if it continued to make me feel anxious or nervous, I would know it was my intuition telling me to slow down, step back, and reevaluate the situation.

Making Friends with Your Fear

All of us have been put in a position where we are forced to make a decision regarding the future of a relationship. Often, we stop and say things like, "I'm not sure if I'm willing to take that risk."

Next time that happens in your relationship, how about turning it around? The minute you feel that you are on edge, fearful and anxious, stop and talk to the fear directly. Here's what I want you to say, although you can phrase it as you please:

"Hi fear. I know that you come to me to protect me, and I understand that. But, guess what? I am not going to let you run my life."

Make friends with your fear. Acknowledge it, thank it, and let it go. For anything you resist only grows stronger.

Trust your observations and intuitive responses and you will never have to live in fear.

Repeat this to yourself often: "I refuse to live in fear."

Hidden Holes

"Autobiography in Five Chapters," from *The Tibetan Book of Living and Dying*, Sogyal Rinpoche (HarperCollins, 1992):

I.   I walk down the street.
     There is a deep hole in the sidewalk.

I fall in.
I am lost ... I am hopeless.
It isn't my fault.
It takes forever to find a way out.

II.   I walk down the same street.
There is a deep hole in the sidewalk.
I pretend I don't see it.
I fall in again.
I can't believe I'm in the same place.
But it isn't my fault.
It still takes a long time to get out.

III. I walk down the same street.
There is a deep hole in the sidewalk.
I see it is there.
I still fall in ... it's a habit.
My eyes are open.
I know where I am.
It is my fault.
I get out immediately.

IV. I walk down the same street.
There is a deep hole in the sidewalk.
I walk around it.

V.   I walk down another street.

This is one of my favorite passages from *The Tibetan Book of Living and Dying*. It really made me contemplate the idea of needing chapter five. After all, if we figured out the problem, faced our fears, admitted our faults, and found a solution, why would we need another street? Well, during a meditation, it dawned on me that even if you have solved the situation and learned the lesson, that sometimes you must let it go and move past the problem completely. What stopped us from doing that in the first place? Habit.

Sigmund Freud said that there are only two ways we can relive our past: our memories and our actions. So much of our fear and anxiety comes from our own reactions to problems. "Is it just fear that keeps me stuck in a rut in my relationships, in my life?" is one way to move out of this conditioned response to life.

Unknowingly, we have trained ourselves to respond to specific situations in a recurring way and have created a vicious cycle of discontent. Look, the new street may still have holes, but at least they are not familiar holes. When you become aware, you can walk around them, and, ultimately, find another path to travel.

The True Meaning of Forgiveness

From a metaphysical perspective, forgiveness comes from beyond this world. That doesn't mean that we flat out ignore what another person has done. Forgiveness is not saying, well, he's a jerk but I'll let that go. It is not letting anyone off the hook. In fact, it has nothing to do with the other person at all.

Real forgiveness means that we know that no matter what happened, it doesn't affect us. It's about releasing the anger and resentment or guilt that you hold within, so that you can get on with your life. Real forgiveness is asking the Universe to show you that this person isn't doing anything to you, but you are. Without that release, there is no real forgiveness.

It doesn't mean that you go back to an unchanged relationship if you are treated badly; it means that you no longer hold on to the anger, pain, or judgment surrounding that person, no matter how justified you feel you might be. If you hang on, you limit yourself and your capacity to move beyond it. As you forgive, you will flow with psychic energy that will open the previously clogged channels.

We do not allow anyone to break through our boundaries, standards, or principles, but in this place, we can transcend their faults in order that we may live in peace. From this psychic perspective, forgiveness makes you stronger and not weaker, because you are in alignment with spirit and not the mortal physical world. We cannot ask to see the innocence of another soul, but must assume that it's already there. It's not about attacking someone else, or even ourselves; it's about transforming the situation into one that can no longer hurt us, or them.

Whoever hurt you only hurt themselves. If you understand that, then you can take your power back. Place your pain in the care of your soul, because this is where real healing begins. Forgiveness will always be an act of the soul. By remembering who you truly are, forgiveness serves you to become what your heart desires you to be. When you find your true worth within yourself, no one can harm you.

Forgiveness activates the intuition and reveals a bigger picture. Once you remember who you are and believe in this natural ability to guide your life, you see the past differently: as a valuable lesson that can transform your life.

State the following:

I forgive you for teaching me _____. *I forgive you and I release you.*

As Rumi said, "It's a habit of yours to walk slowly. You hold a grudge for years. With such heaviness, how can you be modest? With such attachments, do you expect to arrive anywhere?"

Call In the Troops

In the same way we telepathically communicate with each other, we can also communicate with a higher source. If you are in doubt about any aspect of your life—most especially when it concerns our hidden fears—ask your angels, your guides, or go directly to a higher source.

The first time I did this exercise was early on in my life. I had just learned to meditate. One thing I knew was that I had a really hard time with relationships and men. I seemed to keep meeting and dating the wrong ones, and the relationship would inevitably fizzle and die. Or I would end up in a relationship that did last, but only because I already knew it wasn't going to go anywhere near a serious commitment.

I was afraid to let a man in, to let him see the real me. If I told him too much and opened my heart, what usually happened is the information got used against me. Instead of figuring out why, I closed my heart completely. Well, what did that do? It made me even less attractive, because now I came off like a cold bitch. When no one reacted to that in a positive way (and who would?), I got mad. Now I was a cold *and* angry bitch. Lovely. I was just looking for another way to run away and hide and make sure that my relationships didn't actually work, which of course, they didn't.

I got into a deep meditative state and asked my guide why I couldn't seem to have a successful relationship. The answer I got really shocked me. I heard my guide say, "There is no reason for you to be in a happy relationship. For you there is no such thing." Wow. When I tried to figure out where this came from, I realized I had this picture in my mind of my childhood. I witnessed my mother being beaten down psychologically, afforded little or no independence. I associated this with marriage and so, unconsciously, never wanted to get married.

When I dug a little further, many more issues from my childhood arose, issues that involved sexual abuse. Again, this was something I had hidden deep within my mind. Well, that was more than I could handle. But before I took myself to a really good therapist, I kept going. I said to the Universe, "Listen, a lot of women my age find it hard to find a really great guy who isn't taken, gay, a confirmed bachelor, or just plain weird." The answer I got back: "Well, you certainly don't like men, do you?"

Don't like men?! Now that was more than I would put up with! I was in a relationship at the time, and although I had no intentions of committing, I really liked the man. At least, I thought I did.

You know there's a saying that the truth shall set you free. Yes, I get it. It does. But first it makes you mad as hell. So, after I finished being furious, I could see that what I thought I was angry about—all the men who came and went in my life—didn't have anything to do with it. It was what *I* was doing. Not them. Me, who thought I was nothing but damaged goods.

A shadow from the past had been glued to my side. And I not only took it everywhere I went, I projected it onto every guy I met. So when he said, "I really can't see you tonight after all," I would act as if he stabbed me in the heart and then kicked me down the stairs. Such a deep depression would come over me. Here was another man who thought I didn't matter. Now I could see that I wasn't thinking about what the man in front of me felt, but about what I felt.

Unfortunately, in order to get that lesson, I had to keep experiencing this same scenario over and over again. Sure, the names and faces changed, but only when I finally owned up to it and said, "Yes, I get it. I really get it!" did it stop happening. Not because the men changed, but because I did. Once I understood that I could open up, that I could be vulnerable and let down my emotional defenses with the right person, I was fine.

Examining the past can help clarify many problems, but that's not where the healing occurs. The only way we heal the past is to live in the present. It has nothing to do with the love you didn't get—it's about the love you are not giving. And that love is given to you, by you. Think about it. Somehow or another it comes back to feeling you are not good enough. But really, what does that mean? Someone can be attractive to someone and not to the next person. It's all subjective. Or, as my mother would say, even a tarantula is attractive to another tarantula.

People who are more attractive than others are simply those who believe they are. Maybe they had more positive reinforcement in the past, or they worked on their appearance. It doesn't matter. The bottom line is that they don't care who finds them attractive and who doesn't, they just know they are good-looking. It's their confidence that draws us just as much as their physical being.

Use your intuition to examine your fears, the ones in the past as well as the ones in the present. What are they? Now, use your intuition to dig down and find out where that fear came from.

EXERCISE

Sweet Surrender

Write down on a piece of paper the fearful characteristics within yourself that you wish to see transformed. Own these things by taking responsibility for the dark side of your Sacred Self. Surrender them to spirit.

> *Spirit, super conscious, please locate the origin of my feelings/thoughts of _____. Take each and every level, layer, area and aspect of my being to this place within me. Help me to analyze it and resolve it perfectly with truth. Come through all generations of time and eternity, healing every incident and its origin. Please do it according to God's will until I am at the present filled with this same light and truth.*
>
> *I chose being _____.*
> *I feel _____.*
> *I am _____.*

Now burn the piece of paper and let it be done. Tell yourself that it is finished and healed. Surrender is the ultimate safety net, because when we surrender, there's nothing left to hide.

Turn Your Back on Other People's Fear

Turn your back on fear. Yes, that's right. Sometimes just turning away from, instead of coming face to face with, unwanted energy stops it from entering into your body, mind, and soul. In a way you're shielding this energy and sending it back to where it came from. Remind yourself that this energy is not coming from you and if you don't want it, then there's no reason you have to let it in.

Whenever you are exposed to intense emotional outbursts that you find uncomfortable, cover your solar plexus (the area around your belly button). Fold your arms over this area. Have you noticed that some children do this automatically? That's because it comes naturally to cross your arms over your stomach whenever you are feeling defensive. It's how we can block whatever negative energy may penetrate us and make us react when it enters our body. If you breathe while you do this, you will naturally keep foreign energy from entering your aura and implanting itself there, making you feel debilitated, tired, upset, and fearful simply because someone else feels that way.

If you aren't consciously aware of absorbing someone else's energy, pay closer attention to your own feelings and ask yourself if these are truly your feelings or someone else's. The depression, fear, or anxiety you're feeling may not be your own. It may be absorbed from someone around you or someone who was intentionally trying to direct it toward you in the first place.

When people say things such as, "You should be afraid, you never know if this guy is trying to use you, or hurt you in some way," realize that this has nothing to do with you, but with someone projecting their fears onto you. Drop it right now. Who knows where they picked up that fear and who touched it before them? You wouldn't take food from a stranger, would you? Don't take their fears either.

Another way to keep another person's energy from invading you is to get out of your own head. Count paperclips, name the colors of everything you see around you, count the tiles on the floor or ceiling. By activating the analytical part of your brain, you will automatically refocus the unwanted energy into a neutral place. By centering on tangible things, you won't get emotionally hijacked by someone else's stuff. In a way, you're detaching yourself from the drama. As an added bonus, it will psychically open your heart center. In this way, you will have easier access to the creative and intuitive channels that will tell you the real truth.

Most people are afraid, and instead of living life fully, they surround themselves with a bubble of some sort. They see what they want to see, hear what they want to hear, notice what they want to notice. The truth becomes distorted because they rearrange it to fit their needs. Being psychic means you only deal with truth, without modifying it to meet your desires or preconceived notions. Listening to your intuition takes your attention. If you must find a bubble, try the following one. It's lighter than air and filled with love. And love always conquers fear.

EXERCISE

Give Your Fear Away

Whenever you feel that fear is stopping you from moving forward in a relationship in any way, shape, or form, go to your sacred space. Close your eyes and put yourself in a deep, relaxed, meditative state. Visualize a softball of light directly in front of you. If a spirit guide or angel or any other celestial being appears within this ball of light, allow it to remain there. This is a ball of pure love and divine intelligence, and it comes to you from a higher source.

Now acknowledge your fear and then gently hand it over to the ball of light. If you like, you can say a few words such as, "Please take this fear from me and restore my balance and well-being."

Watch as the bubble hovers, then moves upward into the heavens. Tell yourself you are at peace and allow that peace to permeate your being.

Finally, give thanks and gratitude to the source for removing your fear and taking it back to where it originated.

PART II

SACRED JOINING

The Divine Dance of You, Me, We

If I love myself,
I love you.
If I love you,
I love myself.

—RUMI

4

SEVEN STEPS TO KARMIC CONNECTION

You must acknowledge and experience this part of the universe.
Karma is intricate, too vast. You would, with your
limited human senses, consider it too unfair.
But you have tools to really, truly love.

—KUAN YIN

Karma has gotten a bad rap over time. Most people think of it in terms of good karma or bad. But karma is a Sanskrit word that literally means "action." So karma in and of itself hasn't got anything to do with good or bad, but it is the force within the Universe that helps us learn the difference between the two. So what you may think of as positive or negative may not necessarily be so. You might remember a situation as negative, but when you look back at the original action, you may have learned exactly what you needed to learn from it, and that's positive.

Have you been in a relationship where you just couldn't get past a person's defenses or make them love you the way you loved them? Have you ever had the feeling that you've met this person somewhere before? Based on the power a relationship has over you in these cases, that usually means it's a karmic relationship.

Love relationships contain some of our heaviest lessons in life. That's because they have been knitted around the karma we need to work on. Don't kid yourself, even the best relationships have issues that need to be dealt with from time to time. Whether it's a simple issue of expectations or someone with a wandering eye, every problem is an unresolved karmic concern that spontaneously collided. You were brought together in the first place because of karma and you will stay together, or be torn apart, because of karma. Whether it's a past-life issue or a past-relationship issue isn't the point; the point is that the issue came around to be dealt with at this moment in time.

The only way to understand the dynamics of the underlying karma is to use your intuitive abilities to look into them on a deeper level. I do this by using the Seven Step Plan—one step for each chakra.

Basically, the chakras are vortices, or wheels, of energy found along the spine from the top of the head down to the tailbone. These wheels spin through the subtle energy of your body. All seven of these psychic radio stations extend outward into the aura of a person, enabling us to pick up and send out psychic energy.

Each chakra is like a solid ball of energy in our body. The chakras themselves are not physical, but are aspects of consciousness, in the same way that your aura is an aspect of consciousness. Your consciousness represents everything it is possible for you to experience, from your state of being to your perceptions and your senses. When you feel tension in your consciousness, it will show up in the chakra associated with that tension. For example, when we feel hurt in a relationship, we usually feel it in the heart chakra first. If left unattended, that hurt will then show up physically within that area of the body.

This chakra energy flows through us and also emanates from us. Through this etheric flow we can gain access to information about our consciousness and discover characteristics that will enhance our physical and emotional well-being. It allows us to tune into every area of our being by connecting with our chakras and uncovering the mysteries that lie hidden inside all of us. By doing this, I learn all the underlying details that make up the karma I am dealing with. In a way, it comes down to doing some undercover psychic investigative work.

When we communicate with the chakras, we get down to the heart of the matter, the karmic center of its source. With open, uncluttered chakras, we can form a solid foundation for listening and understanding. By using your chakras, you align with the spirit behind someone's words and actions. You won't critique minor inconsistencies or point out mistakes, because that's not the point. The point is to erase judgment and fear and find the real reason someone acts the way they do. When we do this, surface actions no longer hold credence, as we no longer identify with them, but allow them to float by like clouds in the sky.

One thing to keep in mind, however, is that you may very well figure out all the karmic attachments you have to someone and theirs to you, but if you or the other person are not ready and willing to let the negative energy go, it won't work. So be honest; don't lie to yourself. Karmic issues that get in the way of your relationship—fear of intimacy, responsibilities within your relationship, judgment issues—are very often intertwined. But if you work on the issue at its core level, from within the chakra as opposed to on the surface, it will only deepen the relationship.

The chakra satellites allow us to transmit information not only from person to person, but from the subconscious to the conscious mind, and then from the mind to the Higher Self. Each chakra enables us to access psychic awareness, and by grounding in each one we can obtain profound information that enables us to obtain higher levels of understanding. Such understanding enhances interactions in love and romance. As a result, your connections will feel alive and loving.

First, we must understand what controls each chakra and the characteristics associated with each one. Use the following meditations to focus on each chakra and take a deep, hard look inside yourself or your partner. However the energy center feels to you will guide you into knowing what is going on with the person spiritually, at their core. Your intuition will guide you to the information you seek. If the chakras are all aligned before you sit down to have a serious discussion, the psychic satellite stations can only help guide the way.

As we move into Sacred Joining, both you and your partner will be able to say that you have been to the darkness, seen the light, and with a clean heart and clear mind, can make a new life together.

Step 1:
The First Chakra (Root)—Red

The first three chakras—the root, the spleen, and the solar plexus—all control our physical and emotional selves. As such, they are much fainter than the others and vibrate on a lower energy level. The root chakra relates to our self-awareness. It is the area that controls our survival and stability by connecting our physical body to our place on earth. It controls even our most basic functions, like eating and sleeping and any other necessary skills we need in order to survive. The color red contains life vitality and is necessary to create new things.

If this chakra is overactive, it causes a person to be fearful, self-pitying, self-centered, or insecure. Too much energy here can induce paranoia. If this chakra is not centered, it can cause one to revert back to "survival" mode with their partner, making them feel as if they are in danger of being oppressed or controlled. They often engage in a power struggle on a physical and psychic plane.

If this chakra is under-functioning, moving jaggedly, or shooting off rockets, a person can become unstable, insecure, and out of touch with their body and its basic needs.

One couple I counseled both had issues surrounding the base chakra. Her root chakra was under-functioning and his was over-functioning. She ran away from the situation entirely, while he ignored it by indulging in alcohol. Until they decide to balance this chakra, the battle will continue. They haven't stopped fighting yet.

In order to heal this chakra one must come from love instead of survival. When this chakra is balanced correctly, it creates courage and confidence. A person becomes more humanistic, strong-willed, and honest. Imagine this chakra expanding. See it as a ball of red light moving throughout your body and removing feelings of fear and replacing them with feelings of protection and strength. Calm the base chakra, and allow it to feel safe and secure.

Beneficial Foods: If you are under-active, eat foods high in protein, such as red meat and spinach. If over-active, avoid all drugs, even caffeine.

Affirmation: I am in a balanced state of mind. I feel safe and secure. I am grounded. I see my root chakra working beautifully.

Step 2:
The Second Chakra (Spleen)—Orange

This chakra, sometimes called the sacral chakra, is halfway between the root and belly button and slightly to the left. The consciousness this chakra influences is our emotional state, and more specifically, our self-respect. This chakra controls our success and our ability to give ourselves the freedom to expand our interests. As the center of our emotions, it also creates our joy for life.

It can, when balanced, remove our inhibitions and make us independent and socially adept. We can have a normal sex life and healthy use of our senses. This is what we use for self-care and what gives us the urge to make choices that bring pleasure. In reality, we are here to live in bliss, and this chakra helps us attain this sensation. It is where our spirit can actually experience being human.

If a person has an overly active second chakra, they often confuse pleasure and sensation with love. It can also push one's pursuit of happiness to the point of greediness or addiction. It controls our appetite for sensation of all types, including sound, smell, taste, touch, or sight.

Clients who are obsessed with another person, trying to make them commit by forcing their feelings on another, have a second chakra that is under-functioning and off-balance. In the case of a client named Nikki, she started dating a man she felt incredible chemistry with. Although they never discussed it, she assumed that he was as in love with her, as she was with him. She stopped dating everyone else and set her sights on him. But when she discovered that this wasn't the case for him, she went into denial. "He must love me," she said repeatedly. "He can't be unfaithful. What have I done to deserve that?"

Nikki didn't realize that her man didn't consider the relationship serious, let alone exclusive. A battle ensued. I suggested that she work on her second chakra by visualizing an orange ball of light, the color of a sunset, moving throughout her body and making her feel comfortable and independent of any end results she preconceived. She breathed in the feeling of being healthy and happy from within. She completely detached from her physical senses and replaced them with feelings of pleasure and self-acceptance.

Once she got her chakra back in balance, her anger and jealousy dissipated. She could see that she had overstepped her bounds. If she hadn't done this exercise, she would have suppressed her beliefs that he owed her the same feelings she had for him. By dealing with the core of the issue, she backed off and allowed the relationship to progress naturally.

If your partner is in a place where there is too much second chakra energy at work, you should play music, dance, garden, paint, and cook. Sex with this person is great if love is involved; if not, it is very disturbing to this chakra.

Beneficial Foods: Eat chocolate, fruit, honey, ice cream, pasta. (Yummy!)

Affirmation: I am not my body or my mind. I am a spiritual being who is in this world, but not of it. I love my body for what it is: a vehicle and vessel for my soul.

Step 3:
The Third Chakra (Solar Plexus)—Yellow

This chakra governs wisdom, clarity, and self-esteem. It gives a person the ability to perceive themselves and others in a positive light by increasing self-awareness. When this chakra is clear, we naturally become confident, creative, intelligent, and optimistic. We are also more aware of divine guidance flowing into our lives. A balanced third chakra naturally makes a person more charismatic.

If the third chakra is under-stimulated or closed down, a person will usually develop an inferiority complex. They may also overanalyze situations or become ego-driven and highly scattered. They often can't make a decision about anything. Anxiousness ensues, and they live in fear of the future. Relationships will be draining instead of inspiring. If your partner is tired or overcome by sleepiness, this chakra has shut down. And the only way they will communicate is in a passive-aggressive manner.

If overly active, this chakra tends to make a person ego-driven and self-centered. They become forceful, demanding that you see things their way. Often they come on too strongly, especially in the beginning stages of a relationship, sweeping a person off their feet regardless of how the other party feels. With an overactive third chakra, one's intuition is so closed off that they dive right in without checking to see if there is any water below, and the consequences are often disastrous.

In the case of Ron, he had been dating a woman for a long time, but when he felt he couldn't commit, he broke up with her. She didn't take the news well and began to stalk him. At first he ignored her, but when he went to his sister's wedding, which he'd originally invited the woman to, he knew she would show up and make a scene.

Because he was aware that she might confront him at the wedding, he had been opening his third chakra to use as a shield against her overactive one. Sure enough, he saw her walking toward him before the ceremony. Before she reached him, Ron took a minute to use the energy from his third chakra and put his hand out in front of him, palm facing forward, commanding her intuitively with the light from his third chakra to stop. He didn't even have to say anything. She looked startled and a bit shaken up, but she didn't come any closer.

Then he calmly told her that she didn't belong there and that she needed to let this go. She hesitated for a minute, but when other people approached Ron and he joined them in a lively conversation, he noticed that she had left.

This is a perfect example of the third chakra energy in action. Others will follow your intentions if you use the energy wisely and clearly. To activate this chakra, do as Ron did: gather your solar plexus chakra energy and project it forward, using your palms to direct the energy of your will.

Beneficial Foods: Anything yellow.

Affirmation: I am guided by the divine source. Everything I want and need is coming to me now. I will be shown the way.

Step 4:
The Fourth Chakra (Heart)—Green

This is the chakra of love and self-love. Not the type of love we feel as an emotion, but rather as a point of consciousness. In this case when love is balanced, we feel calm, giving, and accepting of ourselves and others. When clear, this chakra controls our compassion, and we feel the pain and joy and struggle of another person. We can give and receive love unconditionally, for it balances our whole being.

This chakra also connects the lower self to the Higher Self. It controls acceptance, abundance, well-being, trust, prosperity, and good health. It is where we can begin to see how a person really feels about us. An over-stimulated heart chakra cannot hurt you. Genuine love is naturally a good thing.

If the fourth chakra is off-balance, a person may become emotionally unstable and critical, and have a hard time giving and receiving affection. They may act loving but feel resentful while doing so. They may give to others out of obligation rather than out of a genuine sense of goodwill, or act nice because they feel they should, not because they want to. Conversely, they have a hard time receiving from others. If the chakra is closed off altogether, one can become bitter, jealous, or indifferent. People who resonate too strongly with others may worry, obsess, or become codependent.

My best friend was proposed to on the anniversary of the day she and her partner met. She expected it and saw it coming, but when he actually popped the question, she wasn't so sure anymore. Suddenly, she was full of self-doubt and wondered if she was doing the right thing. I did not ask her to go into her future husband's heart, but into her own. We are all psychic, and it is through the heart chakra that we can access this information. Even though she was skeptical, she brought her awareness to the area of her heart and, as I had instructed her to, imagined waves of green, the color of mowed grass, flowing through her entire being, opening her up to spirit.

She closed her eyes and looked straight into her heart. There she saw the two of them, standing before a minister, their hearts joined in rapture as they pledged their love for one another.

Even if you have no particular relationship concerns, working with this chakra is extremely beneficial. This chakra is healing and loving. Imagine a green ball of light extending outward into your aura. Pull in a wave of healing energy, wash it over every cell in your body, healing all wounds and hurts and filling you with love. This is life energy and it will heal all.

Beneficial Foods: All fruits are good, but focus on plums, cherries, and strawberries.

Affirmation: I am loved and lovable. I release the past with love and light, offering and receiving forgiveness. Prosperity and abundance are my divine right. Everything I am and do emanates from love.

Step 5:
The Fifth Chakra (Throat)—Blue

The throat chakra is the center of our knowledge and decisiveness. It is the color of the spirit and relates to self-expression and our ability to communicate our needs, truth, and our purpose in life. The throat chakra allows a person to be telepathic and to develop the psychic ability of clairaudience. For me, it is a lot like listening to a radio. This chakra controls the consciousness of psychic hearing. People communicate telepathically whether they realize it or not. It also allows us to hear a higher voice. When you listen to this voice, the conscious mind will connect with the subconscious and you will always hear the right answer.

With an underactive fifth chakra, we often repress our ability to express ourselves, to be honest, or to listen to what we hear. We may manipulate the conversation to fit our own needs, selectively editing out what we refuse to believe.

The throat chakra is the one that will tell you if you should take another street to get to your destination, take another flight out of the airport, catch an alternate train, or leave the man in your life because you always knew that he wasn't right for you. It's our job to listen.

If this chakra is overactive, people may have problems with self-talk and inner voices. They lack discernment between confusing voices in their head and the small inner voice within. This can lead to mental illness.

When Laura first came to me, she was depressed and sad. Her husband had withdrawn and she suspected that he might be having an affair. Before she jumped to any conclusions, I wondered if she had asked him what was going on. He continually reiterated that nothing was going on, that he was fine. Of course, this only made her more suspicious. I suggested that she connect with his throat chakra to hear the truth. When she did, she discovered that they were having financial difficulties and he didn't want to worry her. Knowing this, she could tactfully bring up the subject. Indeed, he was worried about money and once they both talked about it, she felt better.

The wheel of this chakra is blue, like a sky at noon. Imagine this chakra connecting with your conscious mind, your Higher Self, and your guides and then speak to them. See the light and energy of divine guidance pouring into your mind, enlightening every cell of your being.

Beneficial Foods: Barley, wheat grass, bananas, kelp, echinacea, and ginseng.

Affirmation: I only listen to the voice of my Higher Self. I am a channel that receives this divine wisdom.

Step 6:
The Sixth Chakra (Forehead)—Indigo

This chakra holds the key to mysticism, intuition, understanding, and self-responsibility. It can allow one to see people and places in the future, as well as probable events beginning to form. This is where clairvoyance originates. When in tune with this chakra, a person will have the ability to see auras, chakras, spirit guides, and other mediums that allow them to gaze inside the soul and capture the essence of a person. You will naturally see images of past and future. When using visualization techniques to manifest what we want in life, we open this chakra voluntarily to create the life we wish to live.

Located at the level of the forehead, between your eyes and just above your eyebrows, this chakra is also called the third eye. It helps us follow our soul's path by trusting our intuition. Consequently, we see things from a higher perspective rather than the material comfort of our ego-driven selves.

The chakra also strengthens our intuition, imagination, psychic powers, and dreams by connecting our conscious-ness to the Universe. It does this by directing the pineal gland in our head to pick up images, much like a mental television screen. If there is enough energy at the third eye, pictures and impressions will often appear. It's impor-tant to remember what you are seeing from this vantage point, even if the images are vague. Concentrate on your third eye and gradually a larger picture will appear. Un-doubtedly, you'll see things about your life that you don't see now.

A client named Barbara came to see me several months ago. She had just met a man and they had gone on sev-eral fun-filled dates together. Her question, of course, re-volved around the path the relationship would take. She wanted to know if she had finally met the man of her dreams.

Together we opened her third eye by imagining a wheel of indigo light swirling around the area and then expanding until it encompassed all of her chakras. Next, we turned this large swirling ball into a large screen, just like you would see at the movies. We watched the screen until it faded into black. Here she saw her soul image and his and she intuitively knew exactly what had happened, what was happening, and what will happen. It was all so positive, and I am happy to say that she and her partner are now engaged.

If the third eye is completely shut down, a person loses all ability to imagine. They will over-intellectualize life by staying grounded in the physical world. Logic and linear thinking guide them. They see the world with tunnel vision and don't trust anything that they can't physically prove.

If overactive, this chakra can produce hallucinations, leaving a person feeling delusional. They lack focus and concentration because they are all over the place. They can be prone to nightmares or detaching from reality completely.

Beneficial Foods: Lecithin, Vitamin E, chamomile, and tons of water.

Affirmation: I am always safe and divinely guided. Spirit shows me the way.

Step 7:
The Seventh Chakra (Crown)—Violet

The crown chakra is at the top of the head and rules our self-knowledge and spiritual awareness. This chakra controls the consciousness of spiritual awakening, enlightenment, and wisdom. It is here that our Higher Self communes with spirit, giving us access to purity of thought and inner strength.

When this chakra is open, a person is able to see and understand the deepest mysteries of life. At this crown point, heavenly energy flows into our being, allowing us to look into past lives and see a person's soul history. When this chakra is open, a person knows things without having a reason, tapping into the universal mind and finding information that can be invaluable to anything in their life, but most especially in their relationships.

If this chakra closes or become distorted, a person feels no remorse for their negative actions, often acts superior, and can sometimes lose contact with reality.

If one does not open this chakra correctly, or allows it to become overly stimulated, it can cause psychosis or forgetfulness. This person will become easily depressed, as they lack enthusiasm and inspiration.

Opening the crown chakra effectively takes years of practice. One way I do this is to go into a meditative state and focus on my crown chakra. I then imagine a violet orb of light radiating from it. From within this orb, I release a thin tube that rises up into the Universe. I imagine thick white liquid being poured down through the tube into my body. I keep breathing and focus my attention on this healing white light filling every cell within me until I literally glow with illumination. I actually experience the light of the Universe filling me with all that I need to know and be.

Beneficial Foods: Divine energy. Feed yourself with spiritual knowledge and reclaim the mystical powers of your intuition.

Affirmation: Divine right action guides my every move. All of the answers I need come to me from within.

EXERCISE

Clearing the Chakras Meditation

Whenever I work with the chakras, I like to keep a mirror close by. One of the teachers I worked with in India believed that the mirror acts like a satellite dish and calls in energy. Also, if any energy shoots off of you, the mirror bounces it back and intensifies what you should know. I like to keep one on a table to my right (my dominant hand) about two feet from me.

Now just relax. Instead of doing a normal breathing exercise, I usually take a few deep breaths and then I take a deeper breath and hold it for a few seconds. Our inner psychic impressions increase when the oxygen level in our brain changes. By holding your breath for a few seconds, you actually increase your perceptions. Do this for a few minutes and then close your eyes, breath in and out naturally, and just relax.

With your eyes closed, place your mental energy on the mirror. Now, simply ask that you be shielded from all negativity. You ask to accept guidance only from the light, the Divine, and that all the wisdom and energy you experience will be for your higher good and anyone else's higher good.

Now move your concentration to the root chakra at the base of your spine. Visualize an orb of red light there. Watch as the light goes up and down the center of your body, from the root to the crown and back again. Some say that the *kundalini*—the serpent of life energy—runs up and down the spine, but I also believe it runs through the center of the body as well. Try it. Let the light move up and down, faster and faster, until you feel it open up the kundalini freeway where energy can move freely through you.

Remember: the first, second, and third chakras control the body. They are in charge of your emotions and feelings. They are all about self-love. Tend them well, for they will determine what you attract with the more vital chakras, such as the fourth, which controls your consciousness and is the center of love. The fifth, sixth, and seventh chakras all concentrate on psychic energy and ability. All should be balanced so that they not only function properly, but protect us from becoming overloaded in any one area of life.

When you feel ready, center your concentration on the root chakra again. This time allow the orb of light to stay there. Examine how it feels. If it feels rough, or looks ragged or jagged, soothe it with your mind. Ask what it needs to be healed. If you are not receiving an answer, imagine the orb of light as a flower and slowly peel the petals away. See what is revealed to you in the center. I do not recommend that you open the chakras from the outside, as some old texts suggest; in my opinion this involves the outside world and the ego. By going directly inward, you place yourself in the world of spirit and are opening them from that space. Push outward from all of them, except the crown chakra, which you will want to push upward into the light.

Move upward through each chakra, slowly and deliberately. Repeat the procedure for each chakra. First visualize the color of each running up and down the spine, then allow it to rest in its proper place. Imagine you are inside your body at that point and you can see and feel the chakra spinning, unfolding, and opening wider. Once the chakra is open, push out with your concentration and see what information you receive.

Once all the chakras are open, carefully connect each of the centers, moving again from bottom to top: red, orange, yellow, green, blue, indigo, and finally to violet, where you will allow the light to move upward from your crown into the Universe. This balances all of your chakras and allows you to flow easily with universal laws and life in general.

If you are doing this clearing on a partner, visualize him in your mind and follow the same procedure. Pay attention to which chakra you were able to focus on more easily, which one felt good or bad, which color was easiest or hardest to imagine, etc. Which chakra seemed the weakest or the strongest? The answers to these questions will illuminate many mysteries.

At the end of the exercise, always remember to close the chakras (except the crown chakra, as it never shuts down). Actually, you technically are not closing them completely, as you would lose all of their energy; instead of allowing them to remain completely open, spinning and whirling, they become still and pulsate with internal (as opposed to external) power. If you allow them to remain completely open, you will be vulnerable, allowing anyone to attack them or leach off of them at any time.

There are several methods used to close or shield the chakras. I prefer to rest each one and then imagine myself sitting beneath a waterfall of white or golden energy. It cloaks me with resistance from head to toe, and I always leave this meditation feeling cleansed and refreshed, as well as safe and guarded.

By opening up the chakras, one does become more vulnerable. I usually wait about twenty minutes before going into a public place.

5

SPIRITUAL CONFLICT SOLVING

The agony of lovers
Burns with the fire of passion.
Lovers leave traces of where they've been.
The wailing of broken hearts
Is the doorway to God.

—RUMI

It doesn't matter who you are, differences are inevitable in relationships. This much I know. But as we move into Sacred Joining, we must dance to the rhythm of the song that swirls around you, me, we and learn to handle conflicts as they arise.

Often we are unconsciously creating fights to keep us apart, to induce drama and excitement, or to release tension. What we must do is use our intuition to become conscious of the sources of these conflicts and control our standard programmed reactions. With increased psychic awareness, we can acknowledge our anger, fear, and hatred, and skillfully render a solution.

As Sara and Rob said to me, "We still fight, but now that we are using intuitive techniques, we can sit down with each other and both discover what's really going on. We're secure enough now to know that even if we don't solve the problem, it's still not going to tear us apart." This is an excellent example of two people who see their lives through one set of eyes.

When we move from our heads to our hearts, we find the true meaning of "we." Even though Sara and Rob may not find a complete resolution to a conflict, by maintaining a spiritual perspective, they make each other feel safe without feeling unsafe themselves. They agree to disagree, which avoids attack, blame, and guilt, while remaining patient and kind within their loving bond. They bless and support each other, yet still take responsibility for their own issues. And they do all this without relying on each other to make them whole.

When we explore our problems from this sacred domain, we no longer criticize, judge, complain, pick, or nag. We stop creating false interpretations of what people really said. We no longer filter responses or twist and rearrange them. No true connection exists within those circumstances; if we attack another rather than attempt to solve the issue, resentment flows through our veins, which only serves to intensify the conflict.

Yes, but they made us feel bad! Or, they made us mad! However, the bottom line here is that no one can make you mad. *You* make yourself mad. *You* make yourself angry. Anger is resistance to the way things are at the moment. And the way they are is not the way you want them to be, because you have an attachment to a certain outcome. Staying angry affects everyone and everything. Have you ever noticed that a houseplant cannot thrive when the people in its space are perpetually angry? In the same respect, when we are peaceful and loving, everything around us thrives. When we enter such a state, it often feels as if time stands still, or as if time speeds up. And so do your muscles, your cells, and your spirit.

Preventing conflict comes from pleasure, commitment, perceptiveness, forgiveness, owning up to one's feelings, and giving each other our full attention. When you are in this flow, it's easy to be available, to balance between give and take. When you feel loved and appreciated, it's easy to look past the small stuff. We don't keep things inside that later turn into big blowups, and we have fun together as much as possible. One of the greatest stress busters in my own relationship is the fact that he makes me laugh. All the time. A sense of humor is imperative. We don't need to create dramas out of fear and loneliness. Instead, when an issue arises, we clear the air immediately. Last time I had an argument, I just stopped and asked myself what we were really fighting about. I forgot. It was so silly that I actually forgot.

The unhealthiest thing to do is to deny you are mad. It might be more spiritually correct to say, "I'm angry but willing not to be." In order to release this feeling and move beyond it, you express it and take responsibility for your feelings. Then what could have been an argument instead turns into an important part of the healing process.

A man does not owe it to you to hug you when you want or kiss you when you want. You owe it to yourself. Abundance doesn't come from what you get, but from what you give. So if you feel claustrophobic, or say you feel ignored, you can't deny or get rid of the emotion. Feelings need to be accepted as they are before they can be transformed, and when our feelings are revealed appropriately and then forgiven, we have a chance to heal. If anger isn't brought up, it has nowhere to go. Nowhere except "now here." (Notice that it's practically the same word.)

Your beloved is a precious soul, just like you. And both of you are human. We all make mistakes, sometimes without being aware of it, sometimes in a misguided moment. However, if we create a Sacred Joining, we can create a context of safety, where both parties feel free to express thoughts and feelings in a positive, enlightened manner. "You don't spend enough time with me," can easily be phrased as, "How about a date on Friday night?"

There is usually a positive intention behind all of our behavior. Whether we need to feel validated, loved, affirmed, connected, etc., it helps to realize where we are coming from, or where the other person is coming from, before we lose our cool.

For example, we usually repeat ourselves because we feel we aren't being heard, we withdraw out of embarrassment, we talk incessantly when we are insecure, and we yell because we feel shameful. If we can go beneath the surface to find the positive intention, we may feel less reactive and more understanding. You are brought together in heart and mind as well as your body. Forgiveness and compassion are the key to almost anything in life, but most especially to conflict solving.

No one taught me how to love. I am not a master. I had to learn about it like most of us do: the hard way. And it wasn't pretty, trust me. But what I learned was that

I needn't improve my conflict-solving skills as much as I needed to improve my soul skills. Since this is where your intuition resides, all of the answers will be found there. Once I understood this, I could intuitively move beyond the physical realm and speak to my love from the silence of my heart. Within the quietness and stillness of this sacred space, I could ask, honestly and openly, in all my nakedness, the questions I had. I could share the insecurities that held me back and know that in the midst of this inner sanctuary, he would hear me and I would hear him. And we did.

Then and only then did I speak to him on a worldly level. Funny, by the time I did this, neither one of us could remember what the fight had been about in the first place. We healed apart before we healed together, because we both resolved to find a solution. It took me years to learn to do this. In the past I would have been the first one to shout out something like, "You're wrong," even if the guy wasn't. I reacted from a childhood of having to defend myself, and the only approach I knew was a negative one. It was easier to say, "I really need to talk about our sex life," implying there was something wrong with it already, than to say "I love our sex life, but there are a couple of concerns I have that I would like to discuss." This second approach brings the other person into the situation with you, so you can discover a solution together.

You have a choice to love, but you do not have a choice to learn the lessons that revolve around it. Those lessons are coming whether you want them to or not, whether it's in the relationship you are in now or with your next partner. Either way, you are both given the opportunity to come alive, be authentic, and move into the center of things, where real solutions can be found. Honest communication between two people always brings peace, as it makes us free—free to show our dis-eases and wounds and have them exorcised together. With the right partner you can show them the walls around your heart, and all they will do is help you bring them down. Commitment in a relationship is not just to the other person, but to the experience of this truth. Let the intuitive techniques that follow take you there.

Hidden within your heart is a door. Open it. To become more attuned to yourself, intuitively walk inside. Once you enter, you will find that failure to see our judgment of others as an extension of the judgment we place on ourselves only denies both of you from healing. Running away from someone else's pain is the same as running away from your own.

Life is happening now. Most problems or concerns will not be solved solely by our thinking, but by our unthinking, dropping into silence and allowing answers to surface.

Focus on your breath and just say, "Not my mind." The more we rely on our intuition, the more we will give up false stories and misinterpretations. We also are able to express ourselves more clearly and concisely. And we find our own truth; not someone else's, but our own.

At this point, we are not asking a person to change, but reflecting on our own attachments to what we feel is wrong. We are not even seeking a solution yet, but simply dropping into the stillness of the moment, without expectations and false images. It's the old saying of the more you pursue, the farther away it goes. Peel and peel until you feel the real you. Become aware of what you truly want and need and what you can give to accomplish this. This is how true resolution begins.

Another way I become aware of what hinders me from being open, accepting, and loving toward my partner is to write down my feelings. Journaling becomes invaluable. This is where you take one issue at a time and explore it. For example, if you tend to withdraw, keep a log, noting the situation that tends to trigger this behavior. Ask yourself, "What's going on with me? What am I afraid of? Is there really anything to fear here?" After you've explored this in your journal, you will more easily find a spiritual solution.

EXERCISE

Start a Relationship Journal

When I first started my relationship with my beloved, I also started a journal as a means for reflecting, opening, and deepening my awareness. As an added bonus, I found it also helped me experience the healing power of my connection. I had finally met the man I thought was The One and, quite frankly, I didn't want to blow it. Again. The only thing worse than knowing you blew something is knowing you're doing it again.

This time, I wanted to work through my issues. I wanted, deeply, to understand where I was coming from and why and how this affected me. Most of all, I wanted to use my own intuitive abilities to understand the lessons I was working on and what I was learning from him. Some of it has been kept private and perhaps always will be, but some of it I shared with him to explain to him how I felt. When the time comes to share, you'll know. Your intuition will guide you.

The following is an entry that I let him see shortly after we met. We were in a long-distance relationship and I was experiencing doubts about both of us moving too quickly:

> Here's the truth and nothing but the truth. I have never experienced feelings like this for anyone before. Not even remotely close. Perhaps I have loved, but never really been in love? Maybe that's it, because I really don't get it. I have never, ever, thought about someone all day and all night, for this long. And on top of that, the feelings are intense. Not just "Gee, I wonder what he's doing?" Not that subtle at all. It's more like getting banged on the head every other minute. Not exactly the best analogy, because these feelings are sweet and warm and delicious.
>
> But since I haven't felt this way before, I'm not sure if it sort of dies down slowly or if you just keep going

crazy mad until you are together once more. I mean at some point, I have to start functioning like a real human being again. (Any suggestions here would be greatly appreciated.) I really, honestly, don't have doubts about how I feel, or even how you feel. It's all genuine and real. It's really involuntary. Straight from the heart. I mean, I couldn't not feel this way if I tried. And believe me I tried. It's like it is being directed by some higher force that has come in and taken over my whole mind and body. I know I could meet a thousand other men and not a one of them would do what you did in just one weekend.

Where I get scared and frightened is when I start to think about how long it will be before I see you again. And then what happens when I come back home? We live too far apart. Yes, I know better than to jump ahead, to start worrying about something that hasn't occurred yet, and to stay focused on the present and go with the flow and all that other stuff. But I am having a hard time waiting until a week from tomorrow to see you, to touch you. That's where I start to come apart at the seams. And I know you heard that in my voice on the phone today. But it was only about that and nothing else.

I am really happy I met you. I know you've been through a lot, and so have I, but I also know that we have both suffered enough. It's time to start over, a fresh beginning, where suffering no longer exists. I have played small long enough and need to move into my rightful place, and if that's with you then so be it. I know with all my heart that there are no accidents. I think God knew that if we hold each other's hand, we'll get where we are supposed to go so much faster and climb so much higher than we ever have before. I want you to take my hand, to take my life ... and come with me.

The entry above helped me work through my fears and made me realize that I need do nothing, except allow events to unfold. And be myself. After that, I never questioned the distance between us and knew that when the time was right, it would all work itself out.

Another entry, which I later sent to him, before he left for a long trip, helped me to once again reconcile my own feelings:

Even though I know you won't be gone that long, and it is necessary for you to go, a cloud still crossed over my heart today and left me feeling quite deadened and sad. There seems to be a hole where you used to be and I know that I will find myself trying to fill it with a quick conversation on the phone with you. In the end, at night when I am all alone, all I will succeed in doing is falling into that same hole. Within you I lose myself and without you I only long to be lost again. I will miss you like crazy!

Record how you feel in your journal, without censoring or editing it. Do not dismiss anything, as everything that is on your mind counts. Record your impressions and impulses and your intuitive hits on these subjects. Be willing to notice and write down any and all activity in your mind, even if you find them weird, funny, unusual, bizarre, coincidental, surprising, crazy, stupid, you name it. It doesn't matter as long as you don't disqualify certain events or behavior.

If something is bothering you, simply recording it brings you to a different level of consciousness. So just write down how it made you feel, then try to decipher where these feelings are coming from. Are they originating in your subconscious? From your telepathic communication? From the Universe? Do not force yourself to find the answers. If solutions don't come naturally, then frankly it's a waste of time trying to make them appear.

Fighting Fair

I have always been able to predict the success of a couple, not by how well they get along, but by how well they don't. At some point all couples will disagree. But it's how well they handle the conflict that will ultimately make or break the relationship.

Usually, when two people disagree, they generally aren't listening to each other. How can they if they're both trying to be right? If this isn't the case, then it's because one or both of them has left the room. Talking over each other in a heated debate isn't a good idea, but neither is running away.

I know in the beginning of a relationship, if a conflict came up, I personally had a tendency to run like hell. I did that with my current love, only to discover that his ex used to do it to him all the time. I didn't know that. But there's a big difference between walking away, and walking out. I liked to have some space so I could calm myself and meditate, as opposed to saying something I would regret. We talked about that and now I know that if I need that space, I should take it without leaving the house, and then come back to discuss the issue. He also learned to stop projecting his ex-girlfriend's actions onto me, which is a good lesson for anyone.

No matter who is right or wrong, both people have to stop, take a deep breath, and listen to each other's point of view—hopefully without blowing a fuse while they do it. If you follow this advice, nine times out of ten the problem gets solved immediately. Why? Because you both get to see that whatever it is that caused such a commotion probably wasn't worth fighting over in the first place.

Sticking it out and working through our issues is the only way to solve anything. This has already been said by many different people, in many different ways. What they neglect to mention is that it not only works on other people, it also works on ourselves. Dealing with our own internal conflicts is just as important as dealing with others. If you avoid looking at what's wrong or resist getting angry at yourself, you only cause more of a problem. Meditation is the only way I know to resolve these issues within yourself.

Next time you are having an argument with your loved one, step back for a minute, take a deep breath, and ask yourself the following questions:

What am I really feeling? Am I hurting? Angry?

Am I really asking the right questions?

Did I say I would do something I didn't want to do?

When we approach a problem from an intuitive perspective, it will always be about uncovering the truth. Our Higher Self will shift us back to our spiritual center, where we move into the present, instead of being controlled by old fears. This is the true meaning of "solving" any conflict.

I recently counseled a couple who had been married for several years. Both were struggling with the shortcomings of their partner and were no longer willing to shrug them off by saying things like, "He's under a lot of pressure at the office," or "She's just hormonal right now."

We did a wonderful heart-to-heart meditation together, where the couple was seated across from each other. I asked them both to go into a deep meditation. Using their mind's eye, I had them place a protective bubble around the two of them, a magical bubble that not only keeps them safe, but draws out any discomfort or fear that they might feel. The walls soak in all the negativity. I love this magical place, because behind the walls of the bubble you feel as if you are shielded from all things worldly.

Next, I instructed them to keep breathing deeply, to focus on the warm energy in the center of their chest, allowing it to expand more and more. When they felt comfortable, I asked them to focus on each other, on their partner's neck and shoulders and heart, just allowing their own feelings of love and kindness to collect in their hearts, to move up into their arms and hands, and to then reach out with it to the other person. Each one gave and received simultaneously. There was no agenda, no feelings of anger or pain or even joy and happiness. Just love moving freely between the two of them as they honored the richness of the connection. I let the heart-to-heart connection go on for about ten minutes before I slowly pulled them back, gently disconnecting them and removing the protective bubble from around them.

When they were finished I asked them both to make notes on what they had experienced, intuitively connecting with their feelings, sensations, images, or any thoughts they had. By doing this, they both focused on the love between them. Sure, they had conflicts, but they also apologized for their mistakes and were willing to see the bigger picture—their love for each other. They let go of all of their anger and ego-based judgments and came back to the pure acceptance of who and what they were, not only individually, but as a couple.

The so-called problems they were having revolved around him working late and her wondering if he still loved her and if she still mattered. These were nothing more than dramas they had created to avoid their fear and emptiness left over from the past. On an external level, they would keep one-upping each other with the issues the other person supposedly created. But by entering a connection through empathy and love, they saw the equality already present in their relationship. Bringing them back to the here and now helped them to evaluate what was really going on. True intimacy rests on just being.

Relationships are about two growing, open people coming together to help each other be the best person they can be. If we remain silent and allow someone to blame us, we enable them. If we become angry, we avoid them. But on a spiritual path, we intuitively move from you and me, into "we" consciousness and create a Sacred Joining.

Always release your problems back to the source by repeating the following: "Let the Universe fix this relationship and return it to me. I ask only that the outcome be for the greatest good of all."

EXERCISE

Intuitive Dating

Whenever you feel as if your relationship is sinking, don't sit by passively hoping this will get better before it sinks. Letting the band play on while the *Titanic* sunk didn't do anybody any good, especially the musicians!

Remember: you are a valuable part of this relationship and the only part you can really work on is yours. On a psychic path we never ask that any person or situation change. *We* change. Before an issue reaches a head, set aside some time during which you can become spiritually in sync with your partner. Have a date with your man when he's not there.

Dating alone? Yup, that would be the idea. Who needs him? Well, you do, but for now you can have just as much fun and get so much more accomplished if you just leave him at home. What the heck am I talking about? Once a week, set aside some time to go on a date by yourself. Visualize him in your mind wherever you've chosen to have this week's session. The zoo? A romantic candlelight dinner at home? A walk on the beach? You name it. It's up to you.

As you move through this date in your mind, address any specific issues that arise or that you've been dealing with lately. Ask why it came up, if there are any deeper dynamics at work, and how you should proceed. Also ask if there was anything you were doing that created this problem, or what he did to create it and why.

Ask, Are there any issues that we're not dealing with? What one thing would help us in this relationship right now?

If you don't feel the need to talk to him, try connecting with his spirit guides. It's not as difficult as you may think. Ask if they will join you on the date and then have a brief conversation with them about what's on your mind, and listen to what they have to say. I'm sure you'll get an earful.

The Blame Game

He has a lot of issues. She's holding me down. He's emotionally blackmailing me. This is nothing but a codependent relationship. I think that person is using me.

I hear these words, or something close to them, all the time. But if what these folks are telling me is really the case, and they see the truth of the situation, whose fault is it? We can't attack someone for what we feel they are doing to us, so much as realize that we don't have to stay in a place where we will allow it to happen. No one is guilty; guilt is spiritually barbaric. The ego-based mind has an orgasm every time you feel guilty. Guilt serves no purpose whatsoever. Once you understand that the problem isn't what he's doing but what you are allowing him to do to you, you can move past the problem. If you're tired of getting water in your face, stop standing in front of the sprinkler; blaming the sprinkler and getting angry will not solve the problem.

All of us have suffered, and all of us have made mistakes in our relationships. But the truth is the truth and if we always come to our relationships from this place of innocence, we cannot lose. We will be less tempted to take out those daggers we throw at each other without realizing it, cutting into someone's heart or our own. We will put down our weapons and simply say that commitment is about two people who were innocent to begin with. Here we are no longer looking to blame anyone, but merely understanding that in our forgiveness lies our healing. We can go there together, or alone. It's simply a choice: to choose the commitment or not.

It doesn't mean that you will let someone intentionally hurt you. It doesn't mean that you will ignore their childish behavior, or put up with the games they insist on playing. It means that deep down inside, you will understand that their soul is not doing these things, and doesn't even know how, and if you continually remind yourself of that, then you are more likely to work through the wounds to a more healing, loving place. When you do, you can drop this type of behavior and find real love, which consists of forgiveness and compassion, and nobody blames anybody for anything.

There's an old Zen saying: The willow is green; flowers are red.

And there's another Zen saying: The flower is not red; nor is the willow green.

Keep beginner's mind in mind. Look at everything as if it is the first time, because even if you know it isn't the first time you are looking at it, it is.

Love <u>Does</u> Mean Having to Say You're Sorry

Apologizing is like rebuilding a bridge. If you hurt someone, intentionally or by accident, you must make amends or it will haunt you energetically until you wish you had. But this doesn't mean we grovel or wallow in guilt. We simply acknowledge that our actions were insensitive, unkind, or harmful, and say so. It doesn't matter when it happened, how it happened, or where. Making amends can never be a bad thing.

When we give and receive forgiveness, we enter a spot in our hearts and become a source of healing for ourselves and others. When we hurt another person, we must give something back. But a blind "I'm sorry" doesn't work unless you discover why you did what you did in the first place. Otherwise, you'll lay the blame on the other person, but then you will repeat the pattern with someone else.

Alternatively, you can stay and delve into your intuition by breathing and meditating. So ask yourself what your motivations were. Were you feeling resentful? Did you intentionally mean to harm someone in order to get their attention, or perhaps make them leave you because you were too afraid to leave them?

Several clients of mine have complained about having said they were sorry, yet their partner continued to complain about their past behavior. Obviously, they didn't want to let it go. When this happens, I ask the client to intuitively check in with their partner to discover why they just can't drop the subject. By connecting to their partner's heart chakra, they can then discover what it is that they have missed and can ask telepathically what needs to happen for them to release that old hurt. Here, they can also discover their partner's true motivations for not letting go. A lot of times people hold on to a situation to make the other person feel guilty. Or they may have had many grievances they haven't brought up and this one situation was the straw that broke the camel's back, tipping off many other issues in addition to the surface conflict they keep bringing up. Either way, communicating telepathically and then physically can clear up the situation.

Don't Ask, Don't Tell

Another way to stop the confusion in your life is to stop asking for advice. And while you are at it, stop giving it. Check in with your Higher Self instead of your hairdresser for a change. Intuitively discuss your problems with your own inner counsel.

All of the "What do you think he meant by that?" or "Is that how he should treat me?" or "Do you think he's cheating on me?" questions are just ways of seeking approval for something you think you believe about the situation in the first place.

There's an old saying that claims people only ask for advice when they already know what they are going to do. Countless opinions from others will hardly make matters clearer. In fact, it often makes matters more unclear! If you ask people for advice and they are not enlightened, then you will be stuck right back where you were, on the same level of consciousness. To move to a higher vibration of thinking and healing, you must take a chance, believe in yourself, and have faith in the Universe. Try not to ask, unless you really must, in a case where someone is better informed and on a higher level already. And, if you receive an unsolicited opinion, say "I cancel that."

Now meditate and go to your Higher Source. All of the answers you need lay within you. Praying is how we speak to the Higher Source, but our intuition is how we listen. So before you go to anyone else, take the time to check in with your higher power first. No problem is ever given to a person without a built-in resolution. The answer is there and you will intuitively receive it if you open yourself to it.

What's Not Working and Why

In your own sacred space, first get into a deep meditative state. Now take out a sheet of paper and write down everything that you don't like about your current relationship. Be honest. Close your eyes and write down everything that causes you the slightest bit of unhappiness. What makes you dissatisfied? Afraid? Now take each comment that you've written, breathe it in deeply, and repeat what you wrote several times. Now ask yourself, "What beliefs am I holding on to that caused this to happen?"

Even if you feel that the situation is 80 percent the other person's fault, it doesn't matter. We're only here to focus on the 20 percent that belongs to you. What did you do to cause this? Let the answer come to you naturally. If it doesn't seem to come, ask the question differently. Ask why this situation is occurring in your life. Explore your negativity. Invite it in and give it a warm hug. Ask it to stay awhile, so that you can shed light on it and heal it. Now write down a corresponding belief next to it that sheds positive light on the problem.

I had a client named Cindy who was upset because she would make dinner for her partner, but he continually came home late and then didn't eat it. "He doesn't call or even offer an explanation," she explained. "He just figures it's no big deal."

But it is a big deal to this woman, who made sure that she got home from work on time, lovingly prepared a meal, even visualizing how much fun they would have while eating it, and then had to sit and wait while the food got cold. Meanwhile, a slow burning anger rose up from the pit of her stomach, which she purposely tried to quench to avoid another argument.

By writing down this problem, she can now delve into her deep unconscious mind, and intuitively understand that she is translating the situation into the belief that she wants and needs him to make her feel wanted and needed. The belief that she next writes down in a positive light is that she doesn't have to have this validation from him.

Once she studied and meditated on this new belief, she came to the conclusion that she can now burn this old belief. (Literally, if she likes, since it was on a piece of paper.) She decided that unless he informed her he'd be home at a specific time, she would spend her evenings more wisely, maybe even go out with friends for dinner. Or stay home, and not make dinner for a change. What did her partner do? When he came home late the first few times and asked where dinner was and why she wasn't making it, she simply asked him to figure it out. She didn't get mad or upset or turn it into a night of misery. She just went about her business. Now he's home for dinner more frequently and when he knows he will be late, he calls. Sometimes, he even cooks. All because she dug deeper into her psychic mind and discovered the real reason for her reactions. Not his. Hers.

Another way to ask this is to simply question what you are afraid of. If a woman is upset because the man in her life hasn't proposed, what is causing her to feel that way? When you try to reach deeper, you may come to the conclusion, as I did with another client, that the pervasive fear, which then showed up as anger, came from her own basic insecurities. She felt if he didn't commit to her she would be left alone. That somewhere along the way, he might decide he didn't love her that much after all, or that he may find someone else. That's a pretty insidious belief keeping her chained to her own negativity! Once explored, it can be addressed. And it can be replaced by a positive statement, written in the present tense, affirming her own security that lies deep within.

The Cost of Compromising

Women are usually the ones who mold themselves to fit into a relationship. But commitment is not about holding ourselves back, silencing our voices, or changing who we are to fit someone else's picture. Take a minute to meditate and ask these questions:

Does my partner want to be in this relationship with me?

Do I want to be in this relationship with him?

Does he support me and all that I do?

Does he want to commit to communicating and working through our emotional crap?

And the most important question:

Can I ask for what I want or need without worrying about how he will react?

If you have a hard time answering these questions, ask for some guidance. Call on one of your guides, a spiritual master, an angel … whomever you feel most comfortable with to help you unravel your psychological self and supervise the direction of the answers. You'd be surprised how objective an "outside" party can be, especially when it's of spirit.

One way to do this is on paper. Your teachers and guides are always more than willing to help.

What I do, and I do it often, is run to my computer, because this is where I most naturally write. I close my eyes for a minute, and breathe deeply until I feel calm and centered. Then on a clear screen I simply type "Dear God," followed by the question I have. For instance, when I first entered into a relationship with my love, I typed the following:

Dear God: I deserve to be fully met, deeply loved, and joyous and prosperous in the process. Is this the person I can do this with?

Then I simply took dictation. Type or write your heart out. Allow the stream of words to flow through you naturally, without judgment or evaluation. The words could be completely unrelated, or the sentences incomplete, but don't let that deter you. What you are doing, whether you know it or not, is activating your intuition. Don't interject your own thoughts or ideas on the subject. Just connect and get it all down. Analyze what you receive later. What you are trying to do right now is communicate with the Universe, and the last thing you want to do is get in the way.

When you just allow the answers to come, I guarantee they will be incredibly profound. Trying to judge what you receive while you receive it will only serve to cut off the flow. Also, one of the reasons I use my computer to do this exercise is because the words come pretty fast. And the faster you write or type what you are hearing, the faster the messages will come. You are naturally uncovering hidden insights and accessing information you would not have considered. You may also recognize a pattern that allows you to connect situations or thoughts, so you can see the bigger picture.

Just trust the process and let go of yourself. You will know when it's over because the flow will simply stop. Just go with it. And don't forget to thank whomever you communicated with when it's over.

One word of caution: what you receive is great information, but it doesn't mean that it is an absolute given. That's why you have free will. Don't follow any information if it doesn't feel intuitively right to you. It could be you are misinterpreting what you received. Or it could be you are not ready. Angels and guides can assist you in making decision, but they don't make them for you. The power always remains with you.

Cosmic Communication

Most people will tell you that communicating well is at the heart of a solid relationship. Most women express themselves easily. But many men have a more difficult time not only expressing themselves, but interpreting what exactly a woman is trying to tell them. Men don't have a hint antennae built in them. When you say to a man, "Get a clue," it means that you have to give him one.

Unfortunately, our programmed patterns of fear and shame block these pathways. We listen defensively. Our mind is somewhere else. We tuned in, but turned off. Sometimes we recognize this in others, but usually not in ourselves. Without noticing, we continually interrupt, or turn the conversation conveniently back on ourselves.

There is no one specific way to learn to "correctly" converse on a physical level. You could read a million other books on the subject that will tell you things like relax, listen with the intention of understanding before being understood, don't jump in or give advice until asked, check your motivation before you speak, and so on.

Communication is about communion, which means interchange and connection, not "Can I get some cheese? I need to whine." We must allow someone to speak freely, openly, and honestly without fearing that they will be judged or criticized or put down. When you are listening, really listen and respond when you intuitively know that you can. You will feel it when they take a sigh, or pause in anticipation of what you have to say. In this way, you psychically breathe into each other's thoughts and dissolve into Sacred Joining.

Listen with the intent of understanding. You are there at that moment in time to enter this person's psyche, not to sabotage it. There should be no analyzing, lecturing, interrupting, or defending yourself. There will be time for that later. And whatever you do, don't start talking about yourself. "I know how you feel, because that same thing happened to me when ..." does not support the other person or allow them to speak their truth.

Often we're just reacting out of habit. We become defensive automatically, or our mind wanders because we think we've heard the same scenario before. Be aware of how you are speaking to someone and how you are listening. Slow

Call me or not, but I will still hear you.
Take me out or not, but I will still see you.
Be with me, or not, but I will still love you.

down, listen with all of your senses, and pause before you respond. Empty your own thoughts and take in what they are telling you. Not only will you hear them more clearly, but they will hear themselves more clearly. As a result they will focus on the heart of the matter instead of your reactions toward it.

Intuitively, if you are connecting on soul level, by constantly "reading" your partner, words may not be necessary.

What Do Men Really Want?

The answer to this question is quite simple. Men want what you want. Ultimately, relationships evolve and develop from the same energy, and none of it has anything to do with gender. I think that there are some basic fundamental differences, like a man's need to hunt, etc., but after awhile, when I look at all those so-called "differences," it all comes down to karmic rebounds that come back and bite you. You solve one problem, but in turn set the stage for another. The old stereotype had men protecting women, much like a father protects a child, but that no longer holds true. Inequality of this sort is a prescription for a deadly relationship. That cultural stereotype no longer feeds two equal mates. Men may be from Mars and women from Venus, but together we're from the heavens.

The only way to find *our* way there is to transcend our humanness, our genders—which in the end is yet another way to separate us—and find the soul of the two people involved. If we present ourselves exactly as we are, and stay true to this, we can move past what a man wants or what a woman wants into what *we* want. We see each other as different, but equal.

We do this by allowing the still, small voice within to guide us. The two of you can then look into each other's eyes, listen, respond, and continue to build the special quilt that is your relationship, your life together. We naturally ask who the person is, what they like, if we are understanding them, and if they truly feel loved.

The flow of spirit is within us, between us, around us, binding us together as part of all that is. Surrender to the truth and detach from desired outcomes. Honor the unique individual he is. We are not perfect by any means, but it's being honest about our faults and mistakes that counts. In the end we have no power over others. We can only make plans, make decisions, and make love equally. To love someone is to yield to this promise.

So, what does a man need? The same things we all need. Here's my list:

- Everyone needs to feel supported.

- Everyone needs loyalty.

- Everyone needs an emotional connection.

- Everyone needs to feel special.

- Everyone wants to grow and contribute to their communities and the world.

A man may need all of the above, but so do you! All of
us want the same thing: to have someone look us softly
in the eye, touch us gently, and see into our hearts so that
we can be understood, respected, and find our purpose in
life.

As Thich Nhat Hanh said, "We are here to awaken
from the illusion of our separateness."

When Do You Know You Should Leave?

If you pay attention to your intuition, you will never have
to ask that question. Trouble is, sometimes we don't want
to hear the answer. We can't make someone love us anymore than we can force ourselves to love another. But if
we see no possibility of a future, all we can do is let go. Remember, by divine design, every love picks up where the
last one left off. If this is true, then love never really comes
or goes. It simply is.

No relationship can hurt you as long as you remember this. Otherwise, we try and try to fit a square peg into
a round hole, which only makes matters worse. A partner is not here to fit your needs as you define them; they
are in your life to serve a higher purpose, one that you
both accomplish faster together than alone. If the hot sex
dwindles, the breathless romance fades, so what? It's about
a higher commitment of allowing the person to be who
they are. If you really care for them and put them first,
nothing more would occur to you. If it doesn't work on

I looked outside and saw the storm. The rain drenched him; the wind whipped him. But I couldn't go out there. I would stay inside, close my eyes, drink wine, maybe even cry. But I would stay inside. For I knew, above all else, the storm out there was his. Not mine.

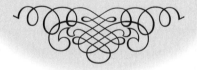

a romantic level, you won't have to make any major decisions. Universal law states that all that is not authentic to you drops away anyway.

So your job is to go for what is authentically you. You give up asking questions like, *What's going to happen next year? Is this permanent? What about our future?* It's not up to you to need to know those answers. Would you ask a girlfriend if she will still be around for you next year? Would you demand a commitment? Stop living in the future. Let a person be and don't try to police them or make them feel guilty.

Relationships are not fixed. When we live in the center of our lives, we follow our heart to do what we are called to do. Life is happening, but where are we? A woman said to me one day that after fifteen years of marriage her husband got up one day, went to the store to buy milk, and never came home. She just couldn't understand it, couldn't even figure out why he did it. But I could. Unless he was the best con man ever, I guarantee that there were signs and clues, hints...*something*. But where was she? Could she not see what was going on? Was she that closed off to her intuitive self that she couldn't see that something was seriously wrong?

All of us want a bond, a connection that is mystical and intangible. Usually we have a picture of what we want the other person to be, how we want them to act, make love, behave, etc. But if we are truly sharing this journey of love, then we can sense and cherish each other's differences and idiosyncrasies. And we know without a doubt when something is wrong. In a Sacred Joining, we drink each other in and are released from worrying about our own needs, wants, and feelings.

The Buddhists say, "Abandon hope." I say, "Just give it up." Same thing. There are certain things you can never change. So does that mean you let a person walk all over you? No! There's nothing spiritual about being a doormat! But we reveal ourselves lovingly, instead of getting angry and not in a way that is making them change. If we come from this space, we realize that even if a man leaves, we are not less lovable.

Ground yourself in the experience not of what you want, but of what is. In that quiet place within your own heart, you can then look into your lover's eyes and ask who they are. Then listen. Really listen. Herein lies a freedom that is beyond worldly concepts.

Axe the Ultimatum

In relationships that work, the love is flowing freely and naturally. You don't have to force it. In fact, that's the worst thing you can do. If you intuitively feel as if you are rowing your boat upstream, then it's time to trust your inner guidance.

A client of mine, Maria, had been dating a man for about six months. She really fell hard for him, and felt there was a deep connection. They both committed to being exclusive to each other. At that point, Maria created a picture of how their relationship would develop, and was anxious to take it to the next level. Clearly, she saw the two of them getting married, and nothing or no one could convince her otherwise. Determined, she developed a so-called plan, discussing it at length with her friends and family, which cemented her attachment. She decided that the next step would be that they move in together and set up house. Without realizing it, or even discussing it with her boyfriend, she deliberately moved in this direction. But he didn't know this and never stepped up to her ideals.

Frustrated, she kept wondering when he would figure it out and propose what she had in mind. She wanted to talk but instead waited for him to initiate the discussion. She was scared, wondering if he might get angry if she brought it up. Besides, she believed that *he* should make the next move. Or was he afraid of commitment like all the other guys she had dated up until then? The disappointments of the past pressed down on her heart.

Had Maria used her intuition, she would have discovered that this guy wasn't on the same page as she was. He wasn't even reading the same book! But she ignored her instincts and plunged head on into "the talk." Upset, she couldn't help but dump all of her pent-up emotions on the poor man. She told him everything she thought she deserved at this point in the relationship. Basically, she let him know that if she didn't get what she wanted, she would move on because she didn't want to waste her time.

A psychic shift occurred, but only in her mind. The mystical third of the Sacred Joining was missing, the "we," because she neglected to see if he was walking through the door marked "marriage" with her.

Like most men, her boyfriend froze. He had no idea where all of this drama was coming from. Where did all of these expectations (which he obviously wasn't fulfilling) come from? He couldn't figure out why she not only flipped her lid, but what he did to make her flip her lid. Maria's boyfriend didn't stick around very long afterward. For one thing, he wasn't prepared for the emotional outburst and wasn't about to wait around for the next eruption.

Later, when she stepped back from the situation, calmed herself down, and centered her spiritual self, her intuition told her that she had blamed him for something he didn't even know he was doing. And she realized she should have discussed her expectations and feelings with him. Finally, she was willing to take off her boxing gloves and stop throwing punches. All her outburst had accomplished was to force him into a fight or flight response. After the dust settled, she was able to go back to him and rationally discuss how she truly felt.

Once Maria intuitively recognized that she was not committed to living a better life with someone she loved, but rather to "getting" her man, she could take back some control. Not of her boyfriend, but of herself. By definition she was being manipulative, and that's highly unauthentic. Then she came to understand that she could be patient, because in the end it was not about getting something, it was about living her life on a higher level.

I once wrote a note to a man that explains why I would never give another man, or anyone for that matter, an ultimatum:

> I cut you out of my life. I wanted you to go. Finally you did. And I wished I could take it back. I felt guilty. I felt mad. No one punishes me more than me. But I let that go now. I can even laugh. I no longer need to do that anymore. Not just to you. But, mostly to myself.

6

LEARNING TO TRUST YOUR INTUITION

What I am actually saying is that we need to be willing to
let our intuition guide us, and then be willing to follow
that guidance directly and fearlessly.

—SHAKTI GAWAIN

If you look up the words *knowing* and *knowledge* in the dictionary, you will find that there is virtually no difference in the intrinsic meaning of the words. They are one in the same. But spiritually, there's a tremendous difference. Knowledge is a function of the mind; knowing is a function of the soul.

To me, knowledge is someone else's theory of what is and isn't so. We hear, see, or read what they say about a certain subject and we form an opinion based on those facts. It's a gathering of information from another source apart from ourselves. Knowledge has its place, but it's not in the realm of the intuitive self.

Knowing is our own authentic experience of what we hear or see or read. Therefore, knowledge creates judgment, whereas knowing doesn't. Bear with me here, it does make sense. If you didn't know that a rose was a rose, then you would have nothing to compare it to. You wouldn't say, "I think it's prettier than a tulip." You feel you love it and when there is no distance, the gap is bridged. When you fall in love with someone there is no distance, because there is no knowledge. You feel a sudden wonder, bliss, a thrill of ecstasy that requires no knowledge of that person.

Once we get to know someone better, we begin to place judgments on them based on the knowledge we are gathering. We create an image of that person and start comparing it to ideas that other people have had, or that we've had in the past, anything that has left a mark in our mind. To some degree, the mystery is lost. That is why a child loves so easily. They have little or no knowledge and with their innocence can look with clear eyes and see only wonder and delight. They have no preconceived prejudices. Children do not try to project onto another person. They come from truth, and not their interpretation of the truth.

J. Krishnamurti said, "To negate is silence." But what was he speaking of? What is it we are supposed to negate? To negate knowledge? To negate mind? Either way, it would require clearing a space within for our Higher Self to commune with us. But you can't negate knowledge with new knowledge; you negate it by replacing it with knowing. When we trust our intuition we are trusting in that knowingness.

Intuition is a natural ability more powerful than you can imagine and it's working for you all the time, gathering information to help you decipher not just your own needs, but those of your partner. When we listen, we beguile someone with our mysticism. It is a tangible, practical ability that can be developed. If, as scientists say, we only use 10 percent of our brain, then intuition is the other 90 percent.

In Sacred Joining, we must understand that the real purpose of love is to help each other grow. We do this by breaking through the walls that keep that love at bay, to find behind it the center of a Universe that lies within each of us. When we listen to our intuition, we will hear our Higher Self helping us move there quickly and without delay. We must honor the voice of the angels, as our real self arises in their presence. You are not only guided, but inspired, protected, and supported.

Psychic guidance is your gift from the Universe. It is your cosmic function. We were able to see before we needed eyes. We heard before we needed ears. And we knew before we needed our minds. Our intuition was given to us to spiritualize not only ourselves, but each other. We are given new minds and new eyes and new ears. I'm telling you, this really works, this looking inside into our deepest core to attract anything you want in the material world. But only through your intuition. So don't take it lightly. You must recognize that these psychic feelings, although highly confusing at times, are of a sacred counsel and should be not only trusted but also appreciated.

When we are receptive to this source of spiritual assistance and conscious of all the planes of energy that it shares with us, then we have a direct connection to God. For those who feel they are romantically impaired, this is a road map to lead them out of dead-end relationships by cultivating spiritual awareness and psychic abilities to create successful intimacy with the one they love. To do this, one must learn to distinguish between genuine intuitive insight and the "wishful thinking" that can easily lead to mistaken choices and unwanted consequences.

When you walk on a spiritual pathway in your relationship, you look at your partner differently. You respond to the person you are with differently. It is the pathway that is built on a foundation of faith. We all have a soul, and when we approach our life from this perspective, we are knowledgeable and conscious of our true nature. We express our divine gifts with everyone we meet and touch. We train our mind to commune with spirit and can open up to seeing (as opposed to looking at) the guidance we receive.

The energy you receive may be subtle, like a feeling, or it may be loud and hard, like a song on the radio or a book falling on your head. The idea, though, is to be open to receive. And that's simply telling yourself that you are allowing this information to come to you. You are already a naturally intuitive receiver just by being born. We recognize this when we remember who we are and why we are here. Remind yourself of the following often—it's what will make the stars in the Universe sparkle just for you:

You are a spiritual being having a human experience.

Meditate daily.

Notice your aura.

Notice your chakras.

Clear your blocks regularly.

Seek guidance from a higher source first.

The mind speaks to us with words, but intuition speaks to us with poetry. Let the song lead you from your head to your heart, because the heart has all the answers.

Some Basic Truths

When you ask yourself the following questions, you just may find out that you are already using your intuition much more than you ever thought you were.

- Have you ever finished his sentences for him?
- Did you know he was calling you before you picked up the phone?
- The last time he was sick, did you instinctively know if he needed to see a doctor or not?
- Have you ever gotten a feeling that he wanted you to call him, or see him, and he did?
- Did you ever experience a sense of déjà vu when you were with him, as if you had done the same thing, in exactly the same way before?
- Did you ever dream of him doing or saying something to you, only to have it happen in real life?
- Did you ever know exactly what he was thinking before he told you what was on his mind?

How many of these questions did you answer Yes to? Have you ever said things like, "I felt the vibes," or "I just winged it," or "We were definitely on the same wavelength." You trusted your gut, which is just another word for intuition. If it helps, write down all the psychic experiences you've had, such as dreams, coincidences, feelings, strange events, etc. I bet you'll find there are more than you suspected.

So, even if you're skeptical about intuition and believe there isn't a psychic bone in your body, you're wrong already. Many of the events that you previously chalked up to coincidence or instinct were pieces of your intuition coming out to play. Now isn't it about time you learned to use it to your advantage?

There are several intuitive channels that you may not be familiar with. Just in case you're not clear on what that might be, and even if you are, it's always a good idea to review.

The primary ways in which we tune into the Universe are clairvoyance, clairaudience, and clairsentience. They are like different instruments that can be played together or separately. Either way, they still make music. Learn to play each one and see what tune sounds the best to you. Harmonize one or more. Just remember that the music you hear is made in heaven.

Most women are clairvoyant. They see things. The literal translation is "clear seeing," and that's exactly what it is, except it's an inner seeing through the mind's eye. You may see images, people, places, objects, or a scene that runs through your mind like a movie.

Although this is the skill that is most prevalent in me, it took years to get there. I visualized and visualized and all I got were fuzzy, fleeting images that didn't really mean much. One day, though, I was just about to wake up when I "dreamed" that I saw myself standing outside in the rain crying, and I was saying to myself over and over again, "How will I learn to live without you? How will I learn to live without you?"

When I woke up, I thought the man I was in love with was seeing someone else, and would leave me, just as I'd seen in my dream. I actually followed him the next Friday night, when he said he had a late meeting. Six months later, he did leave me ... but it wasn't at all what I thought. He died suddenly and after the funeral I stood outside in the rain wondering how I would learn to live without him.

I didn't have many dreams after that, but when I got a flash in a visualization, I trusted it. Shortly thereafter the flashes grew longer and more clear.

Clairaudience means "clear hearing" and is the ability to hear sounds, voices, or music inside your head. Historically, this occurred with angels or the voice of God or spirit guides. But the voices can be from anyone, anywhere, whether dead or alive. My own intuition speaks to me loud and clear. When I ask a question, I don't always hear a simple Yes or No. Sometimes I hear, "Are you kidding?" or "Hell, no!"

Clairsentience means "clear sensing" in French and is receiving messages through feeling. Often, this is an internal sensation, but sometimes it's external. Messages arrive via smell, taste, touch, or emotion. Either way, your body is speaking to you. And not only that, your body knows what it's talking about. Our body and mind are so intimately connected that it is a highly sensitive intuitive channel. A shiver down the spine, goose bumps on your arms, the hair on the back of your neck standing on end—all contain a secret message.

Your intuitive answers will come to you in the manner in which you best recognize them. And the more you trust what you hear, see, and feel, the more the avenues open up. Just remember that everyone is intuitive. There are no exceptions. Just as instinct is an involuntary reflex of the mind, intuition is an involuntary reflex of your soul. We all have it built into us already, all you have to do is access it.

Developing this gift is your birthright. We are meant to listen to messages from a divine source. Our intuition is how the Higher Source, God, or whatever you want to call it, communicates with us. When you pray, you speak to this source. Your intuition is how it responds.

Your gifts are always meant to bring light and love and healing into your life. The answers you receive are born in love, so they will never harm you or coerce you. They come from the essence of your soul.

EXERCISE

Superstar Impressions

You can do this exercise alone or in a group. Either way, I think you'll be surprised just how accurate your perceptions can be.

Cut out pictures of famous men. Doesn't matter who they are, but mix it up a little, like not just George Clooney, okay? How about Dracula, or Einstein, or the president of the United States? Now have a neutral person place each of them separately into an envelope and seal them. Mix up the envelopes.

Now, take one of the envelopes and hold it in your hands. What impressions are you receiving from it? Do the sensations you receive feel warm or cold? Good or bad? Are you sensing a feeling, such as anger, fear, love? Is there a particular style associated with this person? Does a smell come to mind? (Be nice.) Keep going until you no longer receive any impressions. Then open the envelope and see just how close you were to the person you felt you would find.

This is not a "game" in a superficial sense, but is designed specifically to help you become more secure and comfortable with this innate ability, the ability to know things about people, long before they open their mouth.

Developing Your Senses

One of the ways in which we develop our sixth sense is by awakening the other five. Amplify the sounds around you. See things in a new light. If something doesn't smell right, trust your intuition and be aware of the message it is sending you. Pay attention to the energy of things around you. Everything is affecting you on some level and is sending you a message that is either positive or negative. Don't take these messages lightly. Go with your inner guidance.

I had a client who finally opened up her intuitive channels. Once she did, she could no longer watch violence on television, or even watch the news. She was so sensitive to the images and messages that they affected her deeply. The more you evolve, the more these things become apparent. This was an excellent sign that she was moving beyond the physical world and vibrating at a higher frequency. Now she is able to keep the channel open—just not the one on her television.

Yes, But ...

When I first started writing my last book, *Tune Him In, Turn Him On*, somewhere in the process I actually started to believe that it may just be possible for me to find true love. In my early fifties at the time, it wasn't an easy conclusion to come to! I had been left bitter and jaded from relationships in the past, and I was scared. But I really wanted to have love, commitment, and stability in my life. I wanted someone, the same someone to be with, to play with, to laugh with, and to love with. I actually practiced what I preached and followed my own advice.

I believed that we all have a soul mate on this earth. We are all meant to be connected to a certain someone, and I was certain I was still destined to find him. The more I wrote, the more I came to believe that God would not have me do this kind of work and remain alone. Somewhere out there was the perfect partner for me. I didn't set out to find him as much as I prepared to receive him.

Once I decided I wanted a man in my life, I started visualizing what he would be like. Tall, athletic, intelligent, witty, handsome. He was funny and made me laugh, he wrote me romantic notes and left them hidden all over the house, he loved to travel and most of all he really understood me. Maybe he wouldn't be psychic, but he would be spiritual and supportive of the work I do. I could feel that he would be around my age and that he had been married but wasn't now. But from these past relationships, he had come to understand what part he played in their success and their ruin. I longed for this romantic partner and called to him. I really wanted him to show up. I kept visualizing him in my meditation, but never really saw his face. Months passed and no one arrived.

Then one night I had a dream. I dreamt that I was outside on a beautiful, sunny day. I could smell and taste the saltiness of the ocean air. In front of me was a white convertible, and standing beside me was a gorgeous man. We were on a stretch of the Pacific Coast Highway and I could see the ocean and the bubbling waves crashing into the shore. The wind kicked up and blew my hair all over the place. We were laughing and smiling, and I could feel how happy I was. He opened the car door, I climbed inside, and then he bent down, holding his tie against his chest, and shut the door. He came around the front of the car and got in the driver's seat. We sped off along the highway, laughing the whole time. It was amazing.

I didn't know what to make of it. But then I had the same dream the following night and the night after that. I remember telling my girlfriend and my mother that I kept dreaming of this man, but that I didn't know who he was. I could describe him in detail. I said he was tall, built well, and handsome. I recalled that he had medium brown hair that was thick and wavy, but cut nicely in a trim style. The only other thing that struck me was that he had a funny nose, but not an ugly nose. A cute nose. They had no idea what that meant, but neither did I. It's just what I remembered. I kind of thought it might be a business acquaintance more than the love of my life, only because he struck me as being at least ten years younger than me. I just knew that I had a connection with this man. He seemed so real, as if I were recalling something from my memory, not something that hadn't yet occurred. The dreams stopped after that.

Months passed, and I went back to simply calling into the Universe for this special man, even if he wasn't the man from my dream. One day out of the blue, I was speaking to this same girlfriend and told her about a problem I was having with a real estate matter. She told me not to worry, that her husband had a friend who could possibly help me. She said she would have him call me. Well, he did call and left me a message, but I didn't return the call. At that point, the matter had been resolved and I didn't want to waste his time. A few days later, he left another message, but I never returned that call either. Third time's a charm, as he later told me, since that's his limit on trying to reach someone. This time I happened to pick up the phone, as I was rushing to get something to eat before my next appointment. We chatted briefly, and I explained that I hadn't meant to be rude, but I had solved the problem. The conversation didn't end there though. In fact, it never ended. We've been talking ever since.

One slight complication arose: I lived in Northern California and he lived in Southern California. However, by the end of the week, after speaking every night, he decided to fly up to my area so that we could meet in person. When he arrived and I picked him up, I couldn't even speak. This was the man, *the man*, that I dreamt about months before! He looked exactly like him, including the cute ski slope nose. I was so taken by surprise, I froze. Then I told him the truth, and much to my amazement, he didn't run away.

My story doesn't end there, though. When I eventually flew down to visit him, he took me straight to his car, which was parked by his house near the ocean. It was the same white car in my dream, and the wind was blowing and we were both laughing like crazy. How does one explain that? You can't. It's the Universe at work and, as I've said many, many times, if there is a God—and I truly believe there is—then I also know He's much smarter than I am.

Everything was fine. But that's exactly when the "yes, buts," set in. I freaked out. I was used to working with the Universe and always felt supported and helped. Every moment provided me with an opportunity to experience just how miraculous the world is. My invisible barriers were being broken down and one magical moment followed another. Higher consciousness was lighting my way and I had just gotten proof of it. Fear turned into knowingness. At this point, as a practicing psychic, I knew that life was much easier and effortless than ever. It was easy to go into denial.

I second-guessed everything from his career to whether or not he was still seeing his ex-girlfriend. Oh my God, was I ever having a "yes, but" attack! "Yes, but" is just your ego mind trying to take back control. It tries to diminish your awareness and seduce you back into seeing things on the logical surface. What follows is confusion. Your spirit showed you the truth of the situation, but your mind doesn't want you to believe it, because if you do accept what your soul tells you, then the ego loses control. "Yes, but" is a test of your commitment to yourself. Everyone has these attacks in the beginning, but you must trust and have faith in your devotion to your intuitive self. The conviction must permeate our consciousness, for then we have power to rule over our inner world, which in turn creates the outer one. This is the meaning of true enlightenment.

Sooner or later, you have to take that leap of faith. Just leap, and the net will be there. Your soul will catch you. "Yes, but" is fear. Nothing more, nothing less. You will know it is the right thing to do, because your intuition will tell you. You will feel it deep down inside of you in the very center of your being. If you push through, you will be free of the hold of the ordinary restrictions of illusion. A full psychic breakthrough is imminent. "Yes, buts" are the lies we tell ourselves. Truth is the truth, and embracing the truth will get you where your heart desires to go.

To hear the small, still voice within, one must become silent. You must erase the mind. Only when you are completely quiet can the door open. Inside, you will find that you are part of this mysterious presence that knows everything you know, because you become part of it. And, by being it, you know.

The Answer Is in the Aura

Your aura is a field of energy surrounding your body and extending approximately twelve inches in all directions. It's composed of your consciousness—your level of awareness. If a person is fearful, angry, sick, depressed, happy, joyful, spiritually connected, etc., all of this will show in the color and clarity of the aura. Like attracts like, so if you are depressed, you will probably attract and be attracted to someone who is also depressed. It's important to be aware of your own aura, as well as the aura of those around you. Have you ever had a sudden and inexplicable change in mood? If so, it's likely that the person around you spilled some of their aura into yours and caused you to feel this way.

People's auras affect others all the time. Their moods are reflected in their aura and, believe it or not, it will rub off on you. Most of us are just not in the habit of intuitively sensing how someone else's energy can influence how we feel.

I had a client named Lisa who was married to an alcoholic. Most of the time he was either drunk or angry. Lisa loved her husband very much, but because of this, she neglected to protect herself from his "energetic" abuse. This psychic pollution destroyed her aura and left her mentally and physically unwell. Her husband refused to get help, and she refused to leave him. The end result was that Lisa had a nervous breakdown, which is what happens when the aura completely tears wide open. She has since gotten help, which required that she separate herself from her husband until he owned up to his disease and sought treatment. She needed to heal her aura, which could only take place by releasing grudges and forgiving her husband, and then learning to love herself all over again.

In other words, it's not always, "How are you feeling?" but "Who are you feeling?" Another client worked in a woman's prison and didn't think it affected her. However, she became more and more aggressive and angry every day. When I looked at her aura, it was brown and muddy looking. It seemed farfetched to her that she would be so open to this, but really it's not. Her marriage was suffering and the arguments that ensued with her spouse were tearing at her aura and leaving holes in it. (Not good, as this tends to allow even more negative energy to enter.)

I suggested she seek professional help, since she refused to quit her job. But basically, like everything else, tender loving care and self-healing were the key. She felt awful and when she went to the doctor the only thing he suggested were anti-depressants. We worked together to clear her aura and get her back on track. In this case, because of her sensitivity, she eventually found a new job.

When you become conscious of the aura and the different effects of the energy of others, you can easily stop feeling influenced or manipulated by other people. You can take your control and power back, simply by intuitively noticing.

To feel your own aura, rub your palms together and then hold them in front of you about six inches apart. The energy running between your two palms is your aura. How does it feel? Is it thick and sticky? Is it warm or cold?

If you want to see the color of your aura, or anyone else's, stand in front of a mirror, or in front of them. Make sure the lighting in the room isn't too bright, or too dark. Take a deep breath and turn your head slightly to the one o'clock position. Now relax your eyes and then only allowing them to move, look back at yourself, or the other person. See if a color radiates around yourself, or them. Is a color radiating from the person, or you? Is there any debris floating around? Any shapes? Tears?

People who are unaware of their auras can unintentionally let negative energy through. Most commonly the emotions that leak out are filled with fear, shame, anger, or depression. It is important to cleanse your aura often and to protect it on a daily basis, so that any energy that does not support your highest good will be deflected and unable to penetrate your aura.

To cleanse the aura, stand with your feet apart. Close your eyes and on your inhale, imagine all of the debris and gunk in the aura coming to a standstill. On your exhale, imagine it being blown away. Keep doing this until you feel the negativity is gone. Replace that energy with clear, loving light and seal the whole thing in silver. In a way, it's almost like washing a window and letting the light back in.

Color My Aura

The following is a general guide to the colors of the aura and the characteristics associated with them:

Purple: Denotes spirituality and psychic ability. Purple auras are deeply spiritual and enlightened. There is a profound liberation of the mind within this color that allows imagination, inspiration, and intuition to flourish.

Blue: Blue is the color of peace and infinity and is naturally calming, soothing, and balanced. Usually this person is being truthful and honest.

Green: This is the color of healing. People with a green aura are quite charismatic, charming, and endearing. They are secure and self-confident. They calm us in a neutral and positive sense. And they listen well.

Yellow: Yellow is the brightest color and reflects back to us our own intellect. It also promotes serenity and can fill us with liberation and detachment. Because it is so clear, it can also be associated with inner strength and wisdom.

Orange: Orange is the color of the rising sun and therefore makes us more cheerful and alert. People with an orange aura are extremely optimistic and are generally warmhearted. Positive energy exudes from them and they fill you with joy. They are friendly and thoughtful and can inspire others to do great things.

Red: This is the color of physicality. It promotes stamina as well as sexuality. It contains both the fire and sun and so can stimulate love and joy as well as rage and anger.

It can cause the blood to boil and our rate of breathing to increase, or bring us to the heights of desire.

Gray/Black: Those with these colors are often ill or becoming ill. Disease has infiltrated their system. They are extremely guarded and protective. Because of this they are always on the defensive.

EXERCISE

Protecting Your Aura

Imagine that you are standing inside a clear bubble. Now ask the Universe to fill this bubble with beautiful silver light that will remove from your aura all negativity directed toward you or left behind by someone else. Also ask this same light to cleanse away any residue deposited by someone purposely trying to psychically attack you. Ask that this light not allow that person's energy to infringe on yours any longer.

Now release all attachments and return your consciousness to your own energy and aura. Breathe in and see your aura in a crystal clear light. Now imagine yourself surrounded by this same white light. I have a client who surrounds herself in white light daily but always reminds herself to do this before she drives. She says she can feel the layer of protection around her and expands it if she feels another car is coming too close to hers. More often than not, she claims the person in the other car will react and back off.

I also surround myself with blue light when I am nervous, or purple light when I feel I need extra help in repelling negative energy. Practice with different colors and use them as you like for whatever purpose feels right for you. It's one of the first steps to being in control of your spiritual energy.

Always end by filling your aura with love, then slowly open your eyes.

PART III

SACRED UNION

The Spiritual Path to True Love

Is this then a touch? … quivering me
To a new identity,
Flames and ether making a rush for my veins …
My flesh and blood playing out lightning,
To strike what is hardly different from myself.

—WALT WHITMAN

7

SACRED SEX

There is some kiss we want
with our whole lives,
The touch of the Spirit on the body ...
At night I open the window
And ask the moon to come
And press its face against mine,
Breathe into me.

—RUMI

Pardon my language, but my love called me recently and said, "You can't imagine what kind of erection I have right now, just hearing your voice. You have no idea what kind of power you have over me."

Well, that was sweet. But it was also true: I didn't have a clue what kind of power I actually held over this man. That's because I was too busy trying to pretend I didn't care. And, when I did that, he usually responded by trying to pretend he didn't care either. Oh, the games we play. I can't let myself go because he can't let himself go, and then no one lets themselves go anywhere. We remain stuck. But if we stand naked and strong and tell the truth, we can reach heights we never knew existed.

Sex, in its physical sense, is highly overvalued. It has become overemphasized, idealized, exploited, idolized, and cheapened. But this pernicious predominance placed on us by cultural imagery isn't what sex is really about in the first place. That's an act of the physical and has nothing to do with the mystery of the Sacred Union.

Sex is not about taking your clothes off; it's about holding another person's soul in your hands. If we are both truly naked, then our defenses drop and the act itself is merely a deepening of a communication that we have no other way of expressing, except to make love. When that's not the case, sex can lead to heartbreak. But when it is, it only leads us to heaven.

Relationships mean joining, and joining has nothing to do with the body, only with spirit. As we enter into the third stage with Sacred Union, we meet the spiritual third that binds two hearts and souls together, and sex is a part of that spiritual identity. Together, in Sacred Joining, you touch who you really are, as does your partner. It is the ultimate form of expression.

Spiritually, sex cannot be used to create a bond that you are unable to feel emotionally. You cannot confuse sex with love, power, or control. Doing so actually takes you further away from intimacy. Balance comes from being at peace with all of who we are, which includes our sexuality. Making love is an experience of the shared heart that flourishes alongside love and commitment. It flows from knowing each other well and desiring to dissolve into the heart and body of another. That's something you can't learn from a manual of sexual positions.

Sex is a marriage of the heart and soul. It's not a vehicle to get closer together, it's an expression of those who already are close. It is not the wind beneath the wings that help you fly, but the air on which you fly. It becomes sacred when you realize that you can express your love very deeply and without fear. When that kind of honesty is the blanket you lay on in the dark of the night, all you will ever see is fireworks.

Sex, in this respect, is the most healing form of spirituality one can imagine. It becomes an instrument of love and healing, sacred power, and sheer unadulterated bliss. But that's our natural state, bliss. We are supposed to be there all the time, yet only the brave make it. It lights the world from the inside out when two souls actualize a moment in which they are one. That crazy, delirious shock wave that rushes through both of you and touches your heart makes everyone's world just a little bit brighter.

The joy of sex comes from that place. But staying in that place once the sun comes up and the outside world creeps in and we're called back to our jobs and people take us away from this sacred space... that's challenging.

Sex breaks down our walls. It's a mingling of spirit and body, bringing our lives to a meaningful whole. It's an expression of all that we are and all that we can be—our passions, joy, humor, kindness, knowing, and honesty. We love someone so completely that our heart splits open and love gushes out all over the place.

I've heard it all from my clients when it comes to sex. Well, nearly all. But the common themes revolve around two topics: it's over in five minutes (she says), and she always has a headache (he says). Some people couldn't care less if they ever have sex again. They get to the point where they say things like, "Gee, I'd rather stay on the couch and watch television than do *that*."

I embrace your body at night. I embrace your mind by day. Now I can embrace your soul in all the moments in between. At last, I know I am in love.

Some couples use sex to bind back to themselves in times of conflict, hence the wonders of make-up sex. If a problem came up and they felt separate, sex healed and made them feel whole again. But guess what? Nobody fixed the problem.

Sometimes a woman shuts down and does her shopping list while making love. She isn't even with the person on top of her anymore. Others have lost the connection altogether and perform the sexual act out of a sense of duty. Giving and receiving and dissolving into each other's arms have been lost. But I have also met those who make love year after year after year and say it's only getting better and better.

Making love is a natural expression of one body, one heart. We cannot separate sacred sexuality from our bodies—the arousal, smells, moaning, excitement, pleasure, and orgasm. It's spiritually fulfilling, yet remains intensely physical. But if the devotion remains, it reaches a higher level. There's an expansion of energy so powerful that it surpasses our earthly bodies. It's thunder and lightning happening simultaneously inside of you.

Some men know how to love a woman and some men don't. Some women know how to love a man and some women don't. Some know that a light touch of their tongue from the toe to their head, languishing and lingering along the way, tenderly losing its way as it explores the other person's body, can be far more erotic than intercourse. But it's more than the technicalities. It's about the conversation before and during, and about the feelings that intertwine with all of the above. It's about building someone up and telling them how wonderful and precious they are over and over again. It's about kissing them often and caressing them more.

And what does all of that do? It makes us, and ultimately them, surrender into who and what we really are. It doesn't mean we give up or allow someone else to be in control of us. On the contrary, it means that we can both let our strengths run free. That's what creates fireworks.

A younger client of mine, Jennie, was with a man she wasn't entirely crazy about, but she continued to stay in the relationship because she wanted to make certain that he was not the one for her. (Basically, this translates into her feeling afraid to leave, because there might not be anyone else out there for her.) She claimed that they weren't having sex often, but when they did, she felt horrible. I asked her to check in with her own intuition to see if she came up with the same messages that I was getting. She then discovered that she just couldn't say no. She wanted to be adored and loved. I took it a step further for her, and asked if she was sometimes having sex with her partner because she wanted to be polite. Indeed she was.

What Jennie had become was a sexual robot. She was using her body without any soul. It works for a little while, but ultimately it's unfulfilling for both parties. After much discussion and some chakra clearing, her decision was to stop seeing the man sexually, enabling them to realign with each other on a different level.

We all need to be honest with ourselves and with our partner. If we are trying to satisfy lovers in bed by doing things that only please them, we come out of our body and are simply performing an act. Often, this is a result of being afraid to really know yourself sexually, or to become truly intimate with a partner. Psychically, we must learn to go inward, project the person we genuinely are, and stop pretending to be someone we're not. I understand that there's the need to feel good and secure, and to be loved and cherished. So sex answers that question, doesn't it? Sure, until the rest of the relationship rears its ugly head and you're whining to your girlfriends about how bad things are. I know a lot of women who aren't in a great relationship but continually push for a commitment. The sex is good, even though it's not good for the self-esteem. But which one is more important? Hopefully the answer is clear.

Again, the more comfortable we are with ourselves, the more pleasurable it will be not only for us, but for our partner. By opening ourselves intimately together, we also open ourselves to the wonder of all creation.

What's Love Got to Do with It?

Love and sex are not synonymous, especially not for men. Sex is a powerful experience, but it does not—and should not—have the ability to validate you or your relationship. It's the other way around. The relationship validates the sex.

However, if you're good on both scores, you have found heaven. There's something that goes on between the physical world and the spiritual, a natural give-and-take and understanding. Sex thrives on love and love thrives on sex. Real love that comes from giving and knowing and sharing is not a sentimental thing. Love comes from respect and kindness. A delight that glows in everything you do. It's magical. Without some form of commitment, it loses this meaning. It's not a sexual high anymore. That brief moment of ecstasy will be followed by the crash and burn, not unlike a drug addict experiences. The mystical experience has been squeezed out of sex, and it becomes merely an ego-centered machination whose sole purpose is physical fulfillment. If we do this, it's usually at the expense of our own values.

Sexuality in this respect is all about Me. If it is to seek any of these things, then it becomes a biological craving. It's like only having sex for the orgasm, which is such a small part of it. What you've done is turn yourself into objects of desire and nothing more. Emptiness follows. Needing, taking, and grasping rule. We seek to acquire and control. Such questions come up like, Am I doing it right? Does he love me? Will he ever marry me?

After a few hours, the gnawing emptiness is back and the quest for something, anything, to fill our own emptiness arises again. When we don't know how to seek intimacy, we look for stimulation. None of this has anything to do with relationship or coming into awareness of who we are. If we do connect without love, we will feel the consequences, whether we are aware of them or not.

At this stage, men and women alike begin to treat their partner as an object, fulfilling their own needs at the expense of another. We rage inside and then often lash out at a partner, holding them responsible for the emptiness we feel as a result. You cannot fill the soul while emptying it at the same time. Not unlike pornography, this type of sex is an instant fix. You like it because you're in control, don't need to think of someone else's needs, and can live in a fantasy world that has no connection to reality and no challenge to be human. The trouble is you can't compartmentalize your consciousness.

If you are in a sexually open relationship, just make sure it's not because you are trying to fill an unrecognized emotional need through sex. Many clients find they are trying to fill an emptiness inside or are avoiding whatever is missing in their current relationship. In my experience, these types of relationships don't work because they created confusion and disappointment.

Take time to dismantle your sexual drive and find out what motivates you to be sexual. Is it a physical high, a need to be reassured, a release, pleasing him rather than yourself? Notice what and how you feel before, during, and after sex. Sex is sacred; it is not a prison.

Set the Stage

Turn your bedroom into a sacred space. Use it only for sleeping and making love and anything else you find pleasurable. Working in bed can invoke a busy energy in the room even when you aren't working.

Place your bed strategically, no backs to the door or beds crossing entry ways. Do not place the bed against a wall with a window if you can help it. Have a headboard; ones made of wood are best.

Add warm colors to the room, especially greens, pinks and pastels. Blue is too cool and peach is good for finding a lover, but can cause infidelity once you have him. Eliminate clutter. Your bedroom is a metaphor for your mental, physical, and spiritual well-being. Clear the room and you clear your psyche.

It takes devotion to maintain the light of romance. Intuitively decide what you require to set the stage for your spirit to enter. You can spread flowers or rose petals around to bring in the nature spirits. Light candles or burn incense to bring in fire and mystery and passion. Fix special foods and drinks to whet your sensual appetites.

Let Loose

Making love is allowing your creativity and intuitive side to explode. Creativity is breathing spirit back into your soul. It enhances your ability to release your inhibitions naturally and effortlessly, so you are no longer held back by embarrassment and shame. If you approach it as a moment-to-moment experience, which it is, it will be like making love the first time, every time. There is no past, present, or future, there is only now. In the moment, both of you just want to be happy, to give yourself completely, and to feel love.

Bonding together in the present means being there, in it. So whether you're making love, taking a walk, or watching a movie, show up fully, in all of your glory. Stay in touch with exactly what's going on in that moment. The Sacred Union naturally unfolds when we embrace exactly what we are doing. This is truly how you connect. If your mind wanders off, take a breath, go back inside, and come back to the present, the only place where love exists.

Tune in completely to the sensations flowing through you. Be aware of your fingers connecting with your partner, of how your lips and breath intertwine. Delve deeper and deeper, noticing how the sensations change, as if you are experiencing his body for the very first time. Keep looking at your partner. Be aware of tantalizing erogenous zones. Move your fingers just a little bit more. Go slowly, gently, stroking his face, his chest. Allow yourself to bask in the feelings. Be completely in your own body and let it do what it wants to do.

Experiment. I somehow got it into my head one day to try out edible underwear. The entire experiment required an initial investment of maybe ten dollars. So what did

I have to lose? Well, suffice it to say that the whole idea melted into nothingness right before my eyes. (Quite literally, in an ironic way, as chocolate panties and bras don't really have much staying power.) Perhaps I didn't put enough effort into it, or maybe the way the stringed candies reminded me of those stretchy candy necklaces my mother used to buy me when I was a child brought her to mind and, subconsciously, put the kibosh on the whole thing, I'll never know. But it doesn't really matter. At least I went out on a limb, or popsicle stick, to give it a shot.

Give your inhibitions a day off. Let go of anything you use as an escape. Marriage constructs that meant women had to be sexually available in return for security no longer apply. So, no feeling guilty or ashamed. Become a wild woman. And I mean *wild*. Letting go of control isn't such a bad thing, as long as it is for your mutual pleasure.

Kiss your partner as if he were the last man on the planet. Dress up. I had a client named Lucy. She was a newlywed and had just discovered that her husband had a real fetish for costumes. In particular, a French maid outfit (although a police officer was a close second). Regardless, she just didn't feel comfortable getting all dolled up to pretend she was something she wasn't. She flat-out refused. After we spoke, I asked her if her intuition told her it was the right decision, or if she was hiding behind some deep insecurity. She dug deeper, but the only thing she came up with is that it made her feel cheap, almost as if he were making her feel like a prostitute. Understanding this, I asked how she could do what he liked without it making her feel like a paid concubine.

Again, it was her own intuition that explained how she could make this work. Instead of a full-blown costume, she bought a couple of wigs and tried them on with a new accent, which made her feel like an actress instead of a porn star. He loved it! Push the boundaries to the limit and see what happens.

Sexual satisfaction requires breaking out of your "good girl" training, and intuitively connecting with what you really want. Reach down into your psychic mind and into your second chakra to discover your hidden desires. Then use "I" phrases to express them. I want, I feel, I need. Always phrase your wishes in the positive. Saying, "I like it when you spank me, but only when I am reaching an orgasm," is much more effective than, "Don't do that again." (Unless, of course, you *really* don't want him to do that again.) Speak from your heart. Accept praise and compliments. Keep it simple, and above all, listen to what your partner has to say as well.

How to Have a Better Orgasm

You have a better orgasm when you stop trying to have a better orgasm. If we focus on orgasm because there's nothing else bonding the relationship together, the orgasm will never satisfy, no matter how wild or intense. It's the same thing as using pornography to intensify the experience.

You are looking outside yourself to become aroused. If the act itself is devoid of a genuine connection, it doesn't matter what you do, it will never be as good as the same experience with someone you love.

Believe it or not, sex is a part of your spiritual identity. When we are wild with desire and passion, we touch our true core. Dancing with another soul sets our heart on fire, and as we delve within with such abandon, the union of love and sex becomes magical. Sex is not always the ultimate high, but love is; when you combine the two, it's truly mystical.

If you want a better lover, love more. Let go of the awkward adolescent that lived inside of you for so long and become the grownup you are. Try not to let the "good girl" image you had as a child stand in the way of a healthy relationship as an adult. This may sound obvious, but surrendering to powerful, physical pleasure can be difficult when we feel exposed and vulnerable. But when you do surrender, you will be yourself and so will your partner. You'll trust each other more. Do not be guarded when you need to voice how you feel or what you need. Do be caring, responsive, nonjudgmental, and willing to talk. Both partners must be willing to give and receive equally and it's up to you to make sure you are keeping this in balance.

EXERCISE

Sexercises

Improving a sexual relationship always requires learning more about yourself and your partner, whether that's about the physical body or about the relationship itself. Intuitively, we've received messages about power, control, domination, security, or even a sense of duty. Always reveal your true feelings. And remember to tune in to your partner's subtle reactions to everything and anything you say and do.

How much sex you have is irrelevant to the quality of the connection. Here are a few suggestions to strengthen the bond by opening up to your feelings and fears and freeing yourself emotionally. Only then can sex become a full and rich experience that builds on our love.

Feel exactly what is happening to you during sex. Become open and vulnerable to your partner and discuss your fears and inhibitions. Don't hold back. Be absolutely honest and tell him or her what arouses you and what doesn't. Show them. Explore ways to be sexual without doing the deed, so to speak. Touch and massage each other during the day. Be playful sexually without needing a reason. A phone call can be extremely sexual if you want it to be. Slow down and allow the energy to build between the two of you. Stretch your boundaries. Take a shower together. Make love outdoors. Massage each other with oil and wash each other's feet. Change the rhythm of the way you move and touch. Explore, explore, explore.

8

THE NEW "I DO"

I belong to the beloved,
Have seen the two worlds as one ...
First, last, outer, inner, only that
Breath breathing human being.

—RUMI

Some women want to get married, and some women don't. But I wonder, how much of that is a decision we are making because we want it, as opposed to what we are supposed to want? When we get down to the core of the matter, we must all realize that a piece of paper is not what binds two hearts together. So the issue, to me, is not whether we marry or not, but whether the choice we make is what is best for our own higher good. Only your intuition can disclose whether or not a real partnership lifts both spirits.

Ideally, a relationship will be your safe harbor, not your anchor. You can move about with the freedom of who you are, yet still come home. Nothing in life is secure; a bonded relationship provides a dependable home base, a place with loving arms to greet you, and someone to cheer for you as you expand and grow. In a trusting relationship, you don't wake up with a knot in your gut because you are worried that he won't show up after work or fail to carry through on agreements you've made.

A relationship is the place where you can make mistakes, be imperfect, and still be loved. This home base of

The rings we exchange encircle our minds.
The vows we repeat
are written on our souls.
The kiss that seals our union
lives in our spirit for all eternity.
And together, married or not,
we will light up the world.

trust and care helps people feel more confident to venture into new territory, both within themselves and in the world.

Not all relationships attain this desirable state of permanence. Some relationships look more like a feat of endurance than a vital bond that brings pleasure. Some people end up with an agreement to live more as roommates, not lovers. They care deeply but lack the depth that lovers share. I honor contracts, but not if they are tossed around with the self-righteous indication that somehow we are "less than" if we don't adhere to society's limiting (not to mention antiquated) rules.

No matter what form a relationship takes, it can't be about survival. It's a means for opening, reflecting, deepening love, compassion, awareness, and experiencing the healing power of connection. The connection that comes with an enduring relationship is the most powerful healer on the planet, and through it lies a powerful antidote to alienation, stress, and anxiety.

There's a saying that if a butterfly flutters its wings in Africa, it changes the weather patterns in the rest of the world. Every word, every kindness, every touch, every action carries with it an energy that is transmitted to the people around us. Fear and anger change the energy of your surroundings. If we think of our immune system and body as an ecosystem whose health is attuned to our physical and mental environment, then we can grasp the full understanding of the power of love.

There is a stream of life that we must jump into with both feet. When we do, we can feel the rhythmic waves of passion dancing through us and we naturally bring vitality to the relationship and all the people around it. Passion brings with it fire, and fire in this case does not bring death, but renewed life.

As a child, my parents always told me I should find a man I could support mentally, so that he in turn would support me financially. Okay, I never understood that and I still don't. Men are not here just to be supported and if he's holding me back from what I want and need to do with my life, then he is by definition not supporting me. A true partnership is one in which both parties are supported. No one is resisting the other or making them feel less than they could be by quieting their voice and hiding from who they really are. When both people can approve of each other, exactly as they are, they can't help but blossom.

So, the first and only question you should ask yourself about a person is "How do they make me feel about myself?"

You can start with wanting what's best for the other. It's not that any one person should give up anything for the other, but you need a mentality or consciousness that allows you to simultaneously consider both your needs and the best interests of your partner. No one is sacrificing anything, but there is always a give and take, a negotiation of needs, and a trust that our partner wants us to be happy, to grow.

If you are making a commitment because you feel you "should" make a commitment, the falseness will show. On the other hand, if done with loving intent, it shines through brilliantly.

The Myth of Marriage

As a young woman, I was bombarded by dozens of ads and magazines and television shows that made unmarried women feel as if they had a gigantic hole in their lives. None of the men I knew felt this way. They weren't constantly being told that there was something wrong with them if at the age of thirty, thirty-five, or forty, they hadn't marched themselves down the aisle. After all, where are all the *Working Father* magazines? Once I hit thirty, I kept getting asked the same three questions over and over again:

Are you ever going to get married?

Are *you* ever going to get married?

And, wouldn't you guess,

Are you *ever* going to get married?

I didn't get it. There are a lot of people out there who are married and miserable. Gloria Steinem once said, "I have become the man I always wanted to marry." And a lot of women I know are now searching for the man who might be the wife they were supposed to be.

I also find it quite amusing that a lot of the married women I meet are secretly envious of those who are single. Conversely, a lot of the single women are envious of those who are married. And both seem to feel sorry for the other at the same time! *You're single and have your freedom, but you must be lonely.* Or, *You're married and tied to obligations and routines, but at least you have someone in your life.* Well, I come from a different school. Why can't we have our security *and* our freedom?

I realized that perhaps the problem here was not that a woman was single, but that society reacted to her in a certain way. After all, a man who remains unmarried is referred to as a bachelor, while a woman is called a spinster, or worse, an old maid. Could it be that this originates from the fear that an unmarried woman is not controlled by anyone? That she can say or do anything she wants to do? For those who realize just how powerful women are (and this includes other women), that can be somewhat threatening.

Some women put their career first, leaving a lot of men feeling as if she isn't hanging onto his every word, is far too independent, and can actually challenge his own work ethic or career goals. Suddenly, they don't want to be bothered. Actually that's fine; let 'em go. Somewhere out there is a man who won't mind an independent woman. However, part of the problem is that some women don't want to toss the baby out with the bathwater, and want to instead raise that baby. So they succumb to "society" and pretend they are less ambitious in order to have the family they crave.

But you no longer require a husband to get pregnant, and ever so slowly women are coming into their own. A working mother (a bit redundant, don't you think?) *can* have it all, with or without a man.

Originally, monogamy didn't arise from a need for intimacy; the idea perpetuated itself from a man's need to assert ownership over a woman and her offspring. Men often took several wives. This still happens, especially in third-world countries. The point is, if you love and marry, that's great. Lifetime monogamy may suit a lot of people, but if you feel it doesn't suit you, don't let society convince you otherwise.

Take the case of Bill and Irene. They lived together for fifteen years before they finally decided to marry. But they were getting married because they felt stuck and stagnant, not because it felt like the right thing to do. In other words, they were getting married to "fix" the relationship. But that's a lot like making gambling a career in order to get rich—most of the time, you lose what you started with. They weren't considering doing what was best for their partnership. Once they did marry, they had nothing but problems, and eventually split up.

Suddenly, men are more open to change and have been developing their home skills just as women develop their career goals. But the change still comes from us creating a change in our programmed thinking and behavior. We can't change men and we shouldn't want to. As President Woodrow Wilson said, "If you want to make enemies, try to change something." I don't know about you, but I try to avoid making enemies.

It's important to define your relationship in your own terms, with what works for you. Not for your mother, not for your sister, or for your casual acquaintances and friends. You. Based on my experience, marriage comes down to whatever the couple wants to make of it. I've found that the successful ones are those who let go of the narrow, formulaic pictures passed down from society, and instead chose to make up their own rules. They are truly happy.

Creating Your Relationship Affirmation

It's important that you are clear about what exactly you are looking for in a relationship. Use your intuition to determine what will work for you. The trick is that it has to be *your* goal, not your parent's goal, your friends', or society's in general. The form of the relationship should be one that you are comfortable with, one that you can see yourself living in. Being in harmony with your partnership is what will ultimately create a harmonious relationship. This means you have to intuitively delve into your subconscious mind to find the answer. Write down the qualities you want in the relationship and reevaluate them often. This way you will forever be creating a future that flows in a fluid motion. Bear in mind that it can, and will, change. But it should grow along with you, how you feel, and what's right for you and your partner at the time.

Your relationship affirmation should be short, a paragraph at most, and one that will remind you of what is truly important to you in the relationship. Try to express not just what's apparent to you in the physical world, but in the spiritual center of your Sacred Union. This is your own personal motto that indicates your highest ideals. When you get clear on this, the events and circumstances will fall into place to support it. Anything or anyone that is out of alignment with your heart's desires will naturally fall away, and on a deeper, psychic level you'll naturally attract the people and situations that support it.

To help you get started, meditate and try to answer the following questions:

What do I want in a relationship?

What values and virtues am I searching for?

What kind of relationship would inspire me to live for my highest good?

My own personal relationship affirmation changes as my own relationship evolves. But, just to give you an idea, this is where I started from:

> My relationship with my soul mate will allow me the freedom to live my life, and shape my life, and align with my greatest and highest good. I will heal myself so I might heal others. Integrity and honesty in all aspects of the relationship will guide me toward this perfect person, who will ultimately help me deepen my connection with the source so that we both might shine and reflect truth and love back into the world.

Play around and have fun, but in the end, make certain it is right for you.

Real Love Stories

This is about real love. Real love has nothing to do with romance and all the fun stuff that is happening during that stage. It's about the time he accidentally splashes red wine on your Jimmy Choo shoes and you want to kill him. This is about how he whistles too loudly, and slurps his cereal, and you just can't get him to stop leaving potato chip crumbs in the bed at night while he's watching the eleven o'clock news. This is where you get to find out what he's really made of. Lucky you.

Like it or not, how you react under these circumstances will expose who you really are, and who he really is. A successful partnership is based on a mutual trust. In order to achieve that, you have to figure out a kind of language that's all your own, so you can communicate on a deeper level. Which, by the way, will increase intimacy. This is where you must discover what lies beneath the fights and annoyances of daily living and figure out what you are really disagreeing about. Most of all, it's about building a best friendship with your lover.

If we tell the truth microscopically and reveal ourselves deeply, we can then give, share, and make love without holding back, because there is no fear of losing who we really are. This is marriage, with or without a ceremony.

If you really want to know if you can live with somebody, take a road trip together. Do things that force you to see each other exactly as you are. This includes untangling the Christmas lights, and watching his reaction when his baggage is lost at the airport. If you can get through all that without killing each other, it's a good sign. Pick events that intuitively clue you in to what kind of man you may be potentially spending the rest of your life with. One client had her boyfriend take her children to the zoo one Saturday afternoon. Another asked her fiancé to go camping with her and her future in-laws. Okay, camping with the in-laws might be pushing it, but you get the idea.

Is He Interested in a Commitment?

While there's no sure-fire, can't-miss way to tell a man is ready to commit to your relationship, there are a few things that could trigger your intuition in that direction.

- Has he asked about distant events, such as doing something or being somewhere a few years down the road?

- Has he made plans for you to meet his family? It doesn't matter if Christmas is still six months away, he should have said something about meeting his batty Aunt Edna by now.

- When he's talking to his friends, does he refer to you as a couple, saying, this is my significant other or girlfriend, and often speak in terms of we or us, and not I?

- Have you both thrown away your little black books, meaning that names of past partners have been deleted from all computerized devices, which includes cell phones?

- Has he started being around during Monday night football, missed a golf game or two, and become not so interested in boys' night out anymore?

- Do discussions about where this seems to be going cease to exist, because it seems you both just know?

- Has he mentioned a commitment of any kind?

9

HOW TO KILL A COMMITMENT, OR THE NUMBER ONE MISTAKE WOMEN MAKE

You are what your deep, driving desire is.
As your desire is, so is your will.
As your will is, so is your deed.
As your deed is, so is your destiny.

—BRIHADARANYAKA UPANISHAD

When a woman steps into her inner power, she becomes enchanted. In Sacred Union, the inner strength she finds within is what allows her to fully understand that love is never something that comes to us from someone else, but rather is an extension of our own love, reflected back to us through another person. Our lover then becomes someone we stop hiding behind. Instead, it is whom we feel comfortable enough to step in front of from behind the shadows of our own delusions.

If you listen to your intuition, you will hear messages from your soul. And it will not scream out, "Pick me, pick me!" What you would hear is a creative surge of inner knowing. You would hear your heart split open and want to touch another spirit as you would like yours to be touched. You yearn to make someone happy, because it makes you happy and, when it does, miracles happen naturally around you and to whoever enters your life. You would hear that you are already a gift to the Universe and the world, and you are here on earth to love and be loved.

A woman who forgets this about herself becomes desperate. Having lost herself, she has lost her innocence.

She may not even know why, or how, but she is convinced that she is doing something wrong, that she is the guilty party. Essentially, she condemns herself without benefit of a trial. She convicts herself of being less than perfect and proceeds to project this onto everyone else, particularly those she loves. They are not perfect, because she isn't, and then everyone deserves to be punished. Either the bitch in her comes out, or she succumbs to being unnecessarily abused. She gives away her power and voluntarily allows someone else to convince her that she's not good enough, no matter what she does. It's an awful scenario, but it happens much too often.

No matter the current circumstances or past mistakes, it's time to put aside this self-contempt and no longer dwell on what we could, or should, have done. Until we get to the point where we no longer wish to struggle and have had enough of relationships that hurt us, holding on in desperation to what little love we can get, thinking it's the only thing that can save us will kill our spirit and our ability to thrive in a committed relationship.

When you start to believe that you'll do anything for a man, including humiliating yourself or acting foolish, in order to secure his love so he won't reject you, something is very wrong. It's important to stop the self-destructive behavior you will inevitably regret by becoming intuitively aware of each and every action. This means that you stop yourself from groveling, seeking revenge, harassing a man, pursuing him and/or (God forbid) stalking him when he isn't being responsive. This is your ego talking and it's sabotaging your sense of self-worth.

This is when you need to stop dating him and start dating yourself. Get back to your center by treating yourself like the queen you are. Get a massage, pursue a serious spiritual study, erase negativity, refuse to engage anyone who is negative, and get back to your intuitive center. Live in gratitude, pamper yourself, and move into an "I'm okay" state.

Desperation thrives on our feelings of loneliness. We begin to believe we must fill the void, the emptiness inside, with any man who happens to come along, regardless of his bad behavior. Some women would rather be trampled over than remain alone. Remember: spiritually, the void is only an illusion. First of all, none of us are alone. If you live within spirit, you always walk beside a higher source. Being in a relationship with a man who meets your needs will heal this affliction, but to get there, you cannot get stuck in a relationship with a man who doesn't.

Also know that feeling something and acting on it are not the same thing. Feeling desperate is not acting desperate. But, telepathically, he'll feel that vibration coming from you. That need to need. If you feel abandoned, fine, but remember that you are also abandoning yourself. By going back to your sense of self, you will intuitively realign with the clarity and wisdom you innately possess.

Your happiness does not depend on whether a man wants you or not. You're going to be just fine with or without him. If it isn't him, then there's someone better out there for you.

Trust your psychic abilities and the path forward will appear beneath your feet. It's that attitude that must prevail, or you're doomed from the start. Worrying about it, even a little, leaves you sitting on pins and needles, waiting for the next "move." Meanwhile, your interactions start to change, and you start waiting for him to commit. Nowhere in there did you once include making sure that this is the man you really want to spend your whole life with in the first place.

If you're looking for a relationship that will take away your desperation, you are in serious trouble. This is something you truly need to deal with, long before you even meet the person. Being desperate is not going to make you more attractive. I can't imagine any man who is dating a woman and telling his friends, "Gee, I started seeing this really great, desperate woman. I can't wait to see where the relationship goes."

If you are pushing a man to be your one and only, it's likely coming from a need to have things work out exactly the way you want them to. And *only* the way you want them to. In other words, it has nothing to do with the other person. You cannot and should not ever, ever, ever act desperate. Translation, in case we're not speaking the same language: do not get to a point where you will do *anything* for him.

We've all been there, including yours truly. I think I've told everyone already about the time I actually started following a man around and then parked my car across the street from his house, only to discover I had a flat tire.

You try calling AAA without anyone noticing. (I was very young at the time, even though that's no excuse.)

But it comes down to this: when women get desperate, they don't seem to care about their own self-esteem, pride, or anything remotely related to how their actions will look to someone else, or even to themselves later on. So if you're tired of humiliating yourself and looking like a total idiot, here's what you have to do: just stop.

No more groveling, stalking, harassing, or pursuing a man who doesn't have the slightest intention of reciprocating your undying love.

Let me tell you about Elaine. She started dating a man she worked with. Not something she would typically do, but the young man was fresh out of college and had just been hired at her company. At first, he seemed incredibly nice, allowing her to take him under her wing and mentor him. Well, one thing led to another, as they say. She was overwhelmed by her instant attraction to him, as well as his for her. As an authority figure, she liked being the one with all the answers and enjoyed teaching him the ropes. Elaine offered to look over anything he was working on, gave him tips on projects, and pretty soon she was working on whatever he was working on. Meanwhile, Elaine's own position in the company was suffering. She neglected her work, and her family, in order to accommodate her new boyfriend. This went on for months, even after Elaine was reprimanded for the poor quality of her work by her own boss.

In actuality, he didn't need that much help, but she did it anyway, because it seemed to make her feel important, and because it was drawing them closer and closer together. If she was always helping him, he was always with her, always involved. But after awhile, her new boyfriend started getting testy. He would make nasty remarks and become irritable when she asked a question. In fact, when they went to social functions together, he wouldn't have anything to do with her, and introduced her as his "colleague." When she asked him what was going on, he said that he was getting tired of her doing his job for him.

Intuitively, Elaine had not picked up on the fact that she was doing everything and anything for this man while completely neglecting her own life. When I spoke to Elaine, I asked her to intuitively get in touch with his feelings. When she did, she also sensed that he had "used" other women before. I encouraged her to run with her own innate ability and see if this might be true. It was. In the process, she discovered that she was only helping him in the hopes that he would fall madly in love with her.

When we become desperate, we begin manipulating situations and people into loving us. In actuality, this only serves to push them away. Elaine had somehow decided that if she spent more time with this man, he would naturally fall for her. She wanted him to, *desperately*.

All you have to do is make a conscious decision to stop the madness, and the light will appear. Love is no longer about a really great night in bed or a partner who fills the loneliness we feel inside, but about the peace hovering over us, circling us, and calling us back to the person we long to be. The angels find us here and carry us to this place, easily and effortlessly, within an instant. We change. Our patterns and habits change and we become new women. We stop seeking love, in order to find it. As a result, we become kind and caring and stop looking to hook a man we know nothing about. We surrender truly to our feminine self, not because we allow him to be bigger and stronger, but because we're now receptive to our own magnificence.

A woman in love is in her full power. She can do anything. She can have children or not, cook or not, run a successful business or not. We need to be in love. But it starts with our own Sacred Self. It is an experience of ourselves that provides more sustenance than any man could. Yes, it takes work, but, hopefully, you have done that or are doing it now. The payoff comes from knowing that when we reclaim our wholeness, we can have any romantic partner we choose. When your own light shines brightly, the right person cannot help but be drawn to it.

Remember first and foremost: you are a powerful woman. Get that straight right now. Got it? Say it loud and proud!

Being powerful means that you can stand within your center, that you live from your heart, that you have the strength to tell yourself the truth. Being powerful does not mean you have power over anyone except yourself. As Walt Whitman said, "Be not ashamed, woman ... You are the gates of the body, and you are the gates of the soul."

EXERCISE

Have a Counsel Meeting with a Powerful Woman

Who do you think of as a powerful female role model? It could be anyone, dead or alive. Some of the women I think of as powerful, especially when it comes to relationships, are Amelia Earhart, Eleanor Roosevelt, Cleopatra, Bette Midler, Angelina Jolie, my mother, my grandmother, and my great-grandmother. The list could go on and on. The idea is to pick one, or more if you like, to join you in a discussion about men and love and being powerful.

Once you've decided who will join you in the special counsel meeting, find a powerful place to meditate. In other words, do not do this in the kitchen, laundry room, or anywhere else you feel repressed. Your own sacred space would be ideal.

Get into a meditative state. Take nice deep breaths and focus on the rhythm of the air moving in and out. Repeat your mantra, if you like (see p. 253). Now create a cylinder of light just above your crown chakra that connects to the Universe above you. Consciously send your thoughts up the tube and invite whomever you have chosen to be with you to come in. Think of the funnel that you have created as a gateway into your mental house. You are inviting your guest, or guests, to enter into your spiritual house. Keep breathing deeply and remain focused on the cylinder of light. Is anyone coming? If no one has arrived, don't be alarmed. Telepathically call to them until you feel their presence, or sense them standing or sitting near you.

Once they have arrived, and they will, enjoy their energy. Don't be afraid to openly observe what you are seeing and feeling. Now talk to them. Ask questions galore and listen to the answers you receive. You may be surprised at the amazing advice you receive from the person or persons you have asked to guide you.

You Are Power-Ful!

Set a minute aside in your daily meditation to consider and reflect on all of your power—spiritual power, healing power, creative power, emotional power ... above all, your intuitive power. Open the flower of your intuition on a daily basis and breathe in the fragrance of the mystic rose. From the moment you entered this world, this beautiful flower existed. Peel back the petals and inhale the wonder and beauty of this divine scent and you will never be led astray.

Take the time to analyze your power and what it means to you as a woman. In what ways are you powerful? In what ways are you not? As women we can rewrite the definition of the word *power*, if we so choose. We can create it and stand proud in it by simply accepting it. Imagine, then, the miracles you can create.

And, last but not least, reconnect with a sense of entitlement. This is not a negative trait, such as self-centeredness, but rather a sense of self-investment. A woman who feels entitled to be with a man who loves her and wants to share his life with her is not being stuck up or demanding, but self-accepting. Developing a healthy sense of entitlements means creating a positive way of thinking and acting that shows you truly deserve, and have the right to expect, to be in relationships that lift up both parties. I don't care where you have been and what you have done, we all deserve this. If you expect to be treated with respect, you will be.

Signs of Desperation

- Do you find yourself calling the man you are involved with more than once a day?
- If you asked a man to use a condom and he refused, would you still have sex with him?
- Does your life seem to have taken on more meaning because you are seeing this man?
- Do you call your girlfriends to discuss the latest updates with your boyfriend every time there is one?
- If a man is hesitant about making your relationship exclusive, do you insist?
- If a man called you after midnight and asked you to come over, would you go?
- If you just received the opportunity of a lifetime with your job that happened to take you out of town, would you turn it down because your relationship with a man was at a crucial stage and you wouldn't want to risk losing him?

If you answered yes to even one of these questions, go back and read Part I: Sacred Self again. Your mind forgot what your heart always knew.

The Self-Loving Mantra

In the traditional Indian religions (I was born in Pakistan and so I take this definition), a mantra is a sound, syllable, word, or group of words that create transformation. One of my favorite mantras is simply called "I am."

Breathe deeply through your mouth and say to yourself or aloud, "I am."

And then breathe out through your nose and say, "Love."

It has been scientifically proven that one cannot breathe and be stressed simultaneously. It's impossible. So any time you feel a need to get centered, especially when you are with someone you love, return back to your original goal by creating more of the same.

This meditation can be used in many situations, including stressful ones, or ones filled with fear. "I am" should always be said with the inhalation, but on the exhalation you can always replace the word with something else you want or need at the time. I am … calm. I am … loved. I am … well, peaceful, happy, beautiful, rich, healthy, God, Divine.

After you repeat your mantra at least several times, do an intuitive reading on your inner world. Check to see where you need more guidance, or if you need to change something. Whatever you feel now will be a commitment to yourself that you need to make. And only you can do that for yourself.

Edgar Cayce said that we should open to the power of unconditional love before practicing any other skill. If entered into from the perspective of love, the intention can only be for our, or anyone else's, higher good.

BLESS EACH OTHER
AND BLESS THE WORLD

Make me an instrument of thy peace.

—ST. FRANCIS OF ASSISI

Whenever you turn your relationship over to the Universe, you and whoever shares this space not only remain two separate people, but also become part of a whole. It's the ethereal third body that remains separate yet binds both together as one on this mystical, magical journey called life. In essence, you are in love with a partner and in love with life through him.

In the end, we are all here to express oneness, our own unique connection not only to universal energy, but to each other. The world is not healed by one of us loving another, it's healed in an enlightened state, when all of us love each other all the time. If we are all connected and can love each other unconditionally, then we see similarities in everyone, and that unconditional flow will permeate everything you say and do.

When you achieve oneness, you allow your intuition to open a channel between you and the Higher Source, for the only way to allow it into your life is through love. As a conduit for that pure and sacred energy, you will find happiness reflected back to you, no matter where you go or what you do.

Open yourself and your partner to this flow of oneness and allow it to guide your thoughts, your actions, and your perceptions in everything you say and do. In so doing, you can open your heart and look beyond fear, anger, sorrow, and pain. Love is a process that evolves over time, through receiving and giving and knowing and changing and, most of all, growing into who we really are. Love is about being honest with your partner, but also honest with yourself.

When we find unconditional love such as this, we sit in the heart of love. Our actions and thoughts and feelings derive from the purity of the heart of love, and are filled with awe and wonder at everything. Our thoughts and emotions rise and fall as we remain connected to a deeper, unifying force that binds us all together. We become the wave and the water, the candle and the flame. Giving and receiving become one, because as we move into our own authentic self, we understand that we share that same self. It's easier to be kind and compassionate, generous and genuine.

Two people come together to make each other better people, and if they succeed, they in turn make something better for everyone, everywhere. The world is in us and we are in the world. If the center of our being radiates with love, then it reaches everyone we touch in our ever-changing connections. This love does not need to be found. If you seek, you will not find it. This love is something you cannot feel or touch or taste. It is beyond form.

It is you and it is me. When you experience it, you will simply know, because it emanates from the center of who you are. Here we are not only the lover, but the loved and the beloved.

The happiest people I know, whether single, married, or with a significant other, are dedicated to making the world a better place, a more peaceful place, a more loving place. They want to contribute to their community and to the world in general by being the bright, shining light that they are. These people are deeply appreciative. They understand that what they give is theirs to keep until the end of time, but what they don't give is gone forever.

In the end, entering the intuitive heart of romance is all about creating unconditional love and moving in the flow of universal energy. Ultimately, this is the only motivation behind your thoughts and actions. Understanding this before you come into contact with anyone, especially the one you love, will change the dynamics of how they perceive you, and you them. They will respond differently. You will enter into an agreement with your heart open and your defenses down.

The road to happiness starts with you. Only you can eliminate the fears and self-doubt that can wear down a loving relationship over time. Only you can break the destructive habits and relationship patterns that may be keeping you from enjoying a life that is filled with love. I hope women now understand that we are not here to serve a sociological function, that sex is not for procreation alone, and that love has nothing to do with power. We are only here to spiritualize one another, and when we do, both men and women rise to the occasion. We do not grow eyes to see; we see and then the eyes develop naturally. We do not develop our brains; but when higher thought occurs, the brain expands naturally. Our real self arises not from a need to rise higher in life, but from the natural development of our souls.

I hope this book has helped you learn more about your true self. Whether you are moving toward a committed relationship or not, know that if and when you do, if you start with your Sacred Self, you will have a healing, harmonizing relationship that not only saves you, but saves the whole world.

The greatest reward I can ever receive from a client is when they remember who they are. Then I know they can finally begin the journey toward understanding the true magnificence of their souls. In a relationship, the only way to see another's soul is to see your own. The only way to touch another's spirit is to touch your own. Then we will feel true inner peace and be filled with feelings that could melt even the hardest heart. For when we come from a place of wanting nothing more than to experience another person's happiness, as we experience our own, we will know the true meaning of heaven on earth. In the end, this is the only meaning of love, and the only purpose. Love becomes sacred and, when it does, we have found the intuitive heart of romance.

GET MORE AT LLEWELLYN.COM

Visit us online to browse hundreds of our books and decks, plus sign up to receive our e-newsletters and exclusive online offers.

- • Free tarot readings • Spell-a-Day • Moon phases
- • Recipes, spells, and tips • Blogs • Encyclopedia
- • Author interviews, articles, and upcoming events

GET SOCIAL WITH LLEWELLYN

Find us on Facebook

www.Facebook.com/LlewellynBooks

Follow us on

www.Twitter.com/Llewellynbooks

GET BOOKS AT LLEWELLYN

LLEWELLYN ORDERING INFORMATION

Order online: Visit our website at www.llewellyn.com to select your books and place an order on our secure server.

Order by phone:
- • Call toll free within the U.S. at 1-877-NEW-WRLD (1-877-639-9753)
- • Call toll free within Canada at 1-866-NEW-WRLD (1-866-639-9753)
- • We accept VISA, MasterCard, and American Express

Order by mail:
Send the full price of your order (MN residents add 6.875% sales tax) in U.S. funds, plus postage and handling to: Llewellyn Worldwide, 2143 Wooddale Drive Woodbury, MN 55125-2989

POSTAGE AND HANDLING
STANDARD (U.S. & Canada):
(Please allow 12 business days)
$25.00 and under, add $4.00.
$25.01 and over, FREE SHIPPING.

INTERNATIONAL ORDERS (airmail only):
$16.00 for one book, plus $3.00 for each additional book.

Visit us online for more shipping options. Prices subject to change.

FREE CATALOG!

To order, call
1-877-
NEW-WRLD
ext. 8236
or visit our
website

TUNE HIM IN, TURN HIM ON
Using Intuition to Find and Keep the Man of Your Dreams
SERVET HASAN

Use your intuition as the guiding force in your relationships with men—and glimpse the profound power of your soul.

Tune Him In, Turn Him On is a fun, systematic approach to developing your intuition and practically applying it toward finding and keeping the man of your dreams. Refine your psychic and intuitive abilities through exercises and meditations. Determine if your man is lying or cheating. Decode body language, flirt and seduce like a pro, translate man-speak, get him to open up, and anticipate his every desire in the bedroom.

Dishing up expert advice with a side of sass, this illuminating book shows you how to make a date and turn it into forever.

978-0-7387-1560-5
264 pp., 5³⁄₁₆ x 8 $15.95

TO ORDER, CALL 1-877-NEW-WRLD
Prices subject to change without notice
Order at Llewellyn.com 24 hours a day, 7 days a week!

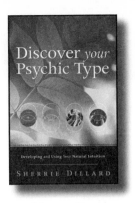

DISCOVER YOUR PSYCHIC TYPE
Developing and Using Your Natural Intuition

SHERRIE DILLARD

Intuition and spiritual growth are indelibly linked, according to professional psychic and therapist Sherrie Dillard. Offering a personalized approach to psychic development, this breakthrough guide introduces four different psychic types and explains how to develop the unique spiritual capabilities of each.

Are you a physical, mental, emotional, or spiritual intuitive? Take Dillard's insightful quiz to find out. Discover more about each type's intuitive nature, personality, potential physical weaknesses, and more. There are guided meditations for each kind of intuitive, as well as exercises to hone your psychic skills. Remarkable stories from the author's professional life illustrate the incredible power of intuition and its connection to the spirit world, inner wisdom, and your higher self.

From psychic protection to spirit guides to mystical states, Dillard offers guidance as you evolve toward the final destination of every psychic type: union with the divine.

978-0-7387-1278-9
288 pp., 5³⁄₁₆ x 8 $14.95

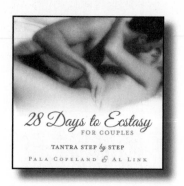

28 Days to Ecstasy for Couples
Tantra Step by Step
Pala Copeland & Al Link

Take your sex life—and your relationship—to new heights in just twenty-eight days! *28 Days to Ecstasy for Couples* can help you and your partner rekindle lost passion, intensify your lovemaking, and experience a sublime spiritual connection.

Perfect for today's busy culture, this step-by-step, illustrated guide to Tantric sex features simple, fun exercises that take twenty minutes or less. Discover how to extend lovemaking, become multiorgasmic, control sexual energy, and engage in sexual, ceremonial, and ritual play. But physical pleasure isn't the only reward. Each activity also includes inspirational messages and lessons in trust, communication, and intimacy.

By practicing sacred love, you'll reap the delights of improved health and vitality and a fulfilling sexual and spiritual relationship.

978-0-7387-0999-4
216 pp., 7½ x 7½ $17.95

THE WAY OF THE LOVER
Rumi and the Spiritual Art of Love
ROSS HEAVEN

The revered words of Jalaluddin Rumi—the greatest love poet of all time—have endured for centuries. His moving verses can help us answer life's greatest questions: What is true love? How can I be more loving? How can love help me grow spiritually?

Drawing on Rumi's writings, Sufi teachings, and shamanic techniques, Ross Heaven presents an utterly unique spiritual guidebook to love and relationships. Your voyage though every stage of the soul is aided by the Medicine Wheel, a spiritual compass that will guide you on "The Path of the Heart." Use this powerful tool to revitalize relationships, uncover fears, resist self-defeating impulses, recover from depression or "soul fatigue," and master the "Art of Love."

978-0-7387-1117-1
216 pp., 7½ x 9⅛ $16.95

To Write to the Author

If you wish to contact the author or would like more information about this book, please write to the author in care of Llewellyn Worldwide and we will forward your request. Both the author and publisher appreciate hearing from you and learning of your enjoyment of this book and how it has helped you. Llewellyn Worldwide cannot guarantee that every letter written to the author can be answered, but all will be forwarded. Please write to:

Servet Hasan
c/o Llewellyn Worldwide
2143 Wooddale Drive
Woodbury, MN 55125-2989, U.S.A.

Please enclose a self-addressed stamped envelope for reply,
or $1.00 to cover costs. If outside the U.S.A., enclose
an international postal reply coupon.

Many of Llewellyn's authors have websites with additional information and resources. For more information, please visit our website at:

www.llewellyn.com